Darina Allen Tim Anderson Dhruv Baker
hard Bertinet Ravinder Bhogal Ruby Bhogal
lerkenwell Boy Anita Cheung Sally Clarke
ady Gennaro Contaldo Ping Coombes
Caroline Eden Chris Edwardes Alison Elliott
us Fergusson Sabrina Ghayour Ravneet Gill
ndy Harris Henry Harris Angela Hartnett
sley Fergus Henderson Margot Henderson
Hom Simon Hopkinson Pooch Horburgh
idge Asma Khan Rachel Khoo Edd Kimber
tiago Lastra Nigella Lawson Jeremy Lee
Rosie MacKean Lisa Markwell Gill Meller
e Oliver Yotam Ottolenghi Nathan Outlaw
o Rose Prince Claire Ptak Rosie Ramsden
Ruth Rogers Ginny Rolfe Vivek Singh
ty Spector Fin Spiteri Itamar Srulovich
ee Tiernan Cyrus Todiwalla
ntine Warner Paul A Young

These delicious things

These delicious things

Jane Hodson
with
Lucas Hollweg and
Clerkenwell Boy

Photography by
Tara Fisher and Patricia Niven

PAVILION

CONTENTS

As with many a good idea, the concept for this book was sparked during a conversation over steaming plates of food, hunkered down on a winter's night around a kitchen table. There were a few of us there that night, although mostly I remember Lucas Hollweg and myself sat at the end of the table waxing lyrical about the visceral energy of food memory. First, you recollect the plate of food, the aromas, the way it looked and tasted, the sensation of it in your mouth – and from there the frame expands to take in the table, the sounds of the place, the people who were present and the entire environment in which that memory resides.

That was early in 2020. Roll on some weeks later, Covid-19 had been unleashed and the country was in lockdown. Suddenly, like many others, I was without the possibility of work and found myself sat at that same kitchen table, staring out of the window and into the gloom of it all.

Throughout my teenage years, I was fortunate to know a kind and wise man, who became both my friend and my mentor. He advised me that in times of difficulty or sadness, a sure-fire way to brighten the spirits is to forget one's own misery and

to apply oneself to helping others. It's a philosophy that raised its head in that moment: I recalled the dinner and the conversation with Lucas – and that's when I got to thinking about putting together a book filled with food memories, each one presented alongside its companion recipe. This would be a cookbook focused more on the story of why, rather than instructions on how to cook – a collective memoir, if you like, written by the shining lights of our incredible British food scene and, with the profits, the very real possibility of helping others.

I went to see Lucas to run the idea past him, to see if he thought it had wings and if so, to ask if he'd like to come on board in making it happen. To all of it, he said "Yes". And there it was – an idea with traction. We sent off our emails, inviting the good and great from the world of British food to be part of our little project. Pretty much everyone we contacted expressed a willingness to help and the stories started to flood in, each one a tale of child-like wonder and deep-rooted comfort.

That's how food memories can grab you. How can anyone fail to be transported by Anna Del Conte's memories of running up to the top of the house to gather snow from the roof with which to make lemon granita? Or charmed by the assurance that Jamie Oliver's first memory was a food memory, as told in the story of his nan's porridge?

Aside from those who wrote their stories, there were some who went one step further... and here I tip my hat to Thomasina Miers, who not only provided a gloriously enriching vignette of her childhood with the story of her family fish pie, but got out her address book and called a few others to join in.

Among her gang was Clerkenwell Boy. On hearing about the project, he picked up the phone to offer his help in making this fledgling idea become a greater tool for raising awareness and contributions for those that really need them.

That's how our idea grew from a tipsy kitchen table conversation to be this book, with all its potential for raising funds for children living in food poverty, so that they are not too hungry to learn.

JANE HODSON

MAGIC BREAKFAST
Ending hunger in the classroom

Morning hunger is a devastating issue that can affect all aspects of children's lives and, shockingly, 4 million children across the UK are at risk of experiencing it. Going hungry doesn't just affect children's nutrition and healthy growth; it also directly impacts their concentration at school and their academic achievements, as well as their mental wellbeing and happiness. Morning hunger can ultimately prevent children and young people from reaching their potential and achieving their dreams.

Magic Breakfast believes that change is possible. That's why we work with schools across the country to deliver free breakfasts to vulnerable children and young people every day. The impact of providing this simple daily meal is astounding. We have seen children in primary school advance by two months educationally, at secondary school young people who regularly eat breakfast achieve, on average, two GCSE grades higher than their peers, as well as incredible improvement in pupils' behaviour, punctuality and social interactions at school. Help us ensure that no child is ever too hungry to learn, be curious and to grow. Scan the QR code to donate directly and to find out more.

Good Mornings

Fiona Beckett

MARMALADE

I sometimes think I must be the only person who writes about food who doesn't come from a foodie background. I remember my late mother's cooking as much for the repellent smell that spewed from the pressure cooker when she was boiling up the dog's dinner as for our own meals: mince thickened with Bisto, overcooked roast lamb with a hefty dollop of mint sauce and Sunday night suppers of cheese and bacon sandwiches made with white sliced bread and Kraft cheese slices.

But her marmalade! Suddenly the kitchen was transformed, filled with the warm, enveloping fug of boiling oranges. I think my mother's recipe came from the *Daily Telegraph*, though I don't have the original, just her instructions neatly written with a fountain pen on a sheet of Basildon Bond notepaper. For years, I didn't make it. I was too busy cooking what I considered to be much more exciting things. Then, in January 2013, the month after she died, I suddenly had the urge to make it again. I have made it every year since.

There's a lovely rhythm to producing it. The recipe involves boiling whole oranges (and a lemon), then sitting companionably round the kitchen table slicing the peel and teasing out the pips. Listen to music as you slice. I've always found that Bob Marley works particularly well, though I'm not averse to a bit of Purcell.

The happiest thing is that I've passed the recipe on to my children and friends, who have loved it and passed it on to theirs. Although it contains shedloads of sugar – marmalade does – I've reduced it from the original, so it's much fresher and tarter than most commercial recipes. I hope you love it, too.

MAKES ABOUT 8 400G JARS (though your jars will probably be all shapes and sizes, so make sure you have slightly more than you need).

1.35kg Seville oranges, preferably organic

1 large or 2 small lemons, preferably unwaxed

1.7-1.8kg granulated sugar (I use 1.7kg)

Wash and sterilise your jars. Not pickle or chutney jars in which the smell tends to linger. The jars need to be as clean as possible. Old recipes suggest sterilising them by putting them in a hot oven, but a run through the dishwasher will do the trick.

Put a couple of saucers in the fridge. I'll explain why below.

Wash and scrub the oranges and lemons and put them whole into a large pan with 1.3 litres of cold water. If you don't have a preserving pan, use a large stainless-steel pasta pan or the bottom of a pressure cooker.

Cover the pan with a lid or a large sheet of foil and bring slowly to the boil. Simmer for 1½-2 hours, turning the fruit occasionally until they are soft enough for you to pierce the skins with the end of a teaspoon. (You can probably remove the lemons after an hour and the oranges gradually after that.)

Remove the fruit and set aside until cool enough to handle. Measure out the remaining liquid. If there's less than 1.1 litres, add water to bring it up to that level.

Cut the fruit into quarters, scoop out the pulp and separate out the pips – don't chuck them away. Cut the skins into small thick slices and add them back to the pan along with the pulp. (You can, of course, cut the amount of work involved by chopping the peel in a food processor, but I like proper chunks in my marmalade.)

Heat up the reserved cooking liquid slightly. Put the reserved pips in a sieve, hold it over the pan of fruit and pass the liquid through, stirring to loosen the pulp still attached to pips. Scrape it off the bottom of the sieve with a spatula. Give the fruit and liquid a stir and leave to rest for an hour or so. This helps improve the set.

Bring the fruit up to just below boiling point, add the sugar and leave over a low heat, stirring occasionally until dissolved. Then bring back to the boil and cook quite fast for 25-30 minutes, this time without stirring.

After 25 minutes, test a little on a chilled saucer to see if it's set. As it cools it should crinkle when you push it with your finger. If it doesn't, boil it for another 5 minutes and repeat the saucer test.

As the marmalade reaches setting point it will darken and grow thicker, but don't overcook it. I like mine light, and as tart as possible given the shedload of sugar in it.

Once the marmalade has reached setting point, remove from the heat, skim off any foam from the surface and allow to cool for about half an hour.

Warm your jars if they're not already sitting in the dishwasher and ladle or pour the marmalade into them (using a funnel makes this easier). Cover with a disc of waxed paper and seal with screw-top lids. Leave until cool before labelling or the labels won't stick.

Feel smug and happy.

Fiona Beckett is a food and wine columnist for The Guardian *and author of several books, including* How to Drink Without Drinking. *Her blog is matchingfoodandwine.com*

Nieves Barragán Mohacho

HUEVOS ROTOS

I grew up in Santurtzi, a small fishing town in the north of Spain. It's famous for its sardines, which is why there are sardines on the logo of my restaurant, Sabor. I love my home and miss it terribly when I've been away for too long.

What can I tell you about my childhood there? Well, we were a normal family: me, my brother, who is 10 years older than me, and my two parents. My mother and father both worked, but my mother also found time to cook. In fact, she was always cooking – and let me tell you, she is a very good cook. Throughout my childhood, we ate this dish at least once, often twice, a week and it is still one of my favourites. It's the kind of dish that is completely satisfying on so many levels and it feels like home. You can eat it at any time of the day – breakfast, lunch or supper. There's never a wrong moment to eat these "broken eggs".

Once everything is on your plate, take two big slices of bread and use one to pierce the egg so the yolk runs out over the potatoes. Make sure you mix everything together and then eat – with your hands. Eating this dish, in this way, always made for a happy and rare silence in our family kitchen.

It's the best dish in the world and so easy to make. Everyone has eggs, bread and potatoes at home. If you don't have Ibérico ham, use any other kind of cured meat... salami, prosciutto, whatever you have. As for how you cook it, my mother has the best attitude and advice: "It doesn't matter what you do in the kitchen," she says, "just pay attention. If you are going to fry an egg, fry it properly."

400g small waxy potatoes, cooked, peeled, cut into ½cm slices

¼ white onion, sliced thinly

2 tbsp sweet vinegar, such as Moscatel vinegar

2 bay leaves

1 pinch smoked paprika

2 eggs

50g Ibérico ham slices

salt and pepper

olive oil

2 slices good bread

Preheat the oven to 200C/180C Fan/Gas 6.

Put the potatoes and onions in an oven pan, splash with olive oil and add the vinegar, bay leaves, smoked paprika, salt and pepper. Mix thoroughly and put in the oven for 20 minutes. Stir every 5 minutes to make sure everything is well coated and getting soft, but not crispy.

Meanwhile, fry the eggs. To do this, make sure the olive oil is 1½cm deep in the frying pan. Heat the oil until it is hot but not smoking, then carefully break in the eggs. As they cook, spoon the oil over the yolks, just three times. This will make the yolks look whitish, but when you dip your bread into it, there'll be a wonderful explosion of colour and flavour, which makes it perfect as it runs over the potatoes. The egg is done when the edges of the white are browned and crispy. Cooking the egg like this is vital to the success of the dish.

When the egg is ready, put it to one side while you make a bed of potatoes on your plate. Place the egg on top with the jamón laid out around it. Grab your thick slices of bread and tuck in.

Nieves Barragán Mohacho was executive chef at Barrafina and is co-founder of the Michelin-starred Sabor in London

Fingal Ferguson

DRY-CURED BACON

My family has been making cheese on the farm at Gubbeen in West Cork since 1979. It was a fascinating place to grow up. During the 1980s, artisan food was starting to take off, and the welcoming arms of my parents received a constant stream of chefs, deli owners, distributors, cheesemongers from New York and London, French students on work experience, young travellers who wanted to learn about cheesemaking, as well as friends and family. The farmhouse kitchen was at the centre of things, with a dog in a basket in the corner and an old range filled with bubbling pots and pans.

My father was up at 5.30am to milk the cows and start the boilers for cheesemaking. The sound of clanking pans in the kitchen was the sign that he was in from his early morning chores and that breakfast was underway. Toast was cooked on a mesh grate over the hot ring, butter applied heavily from the dish in the middle of the table. Eggs from the farm, still coated with little bits of straw, were pulled from a basket beside the kitchen sink and cracked into a pan; the best days were when we had duck eggs with their rich yolks. There was coffee steeping in a large jug, waiting for the grounds to settle, and a sieve to catch the stray grinds. Hung on a hook overhead was a peppered, smoked bacon loin, bartered from Chris Jepson, who smoked our cheeses for us on the coast at his house near Goleen. Dad would lift the slab of bacon down from the hook, take out his old knife, sharpened on a smooth bit of wall outside the kitchen door, and cut rustic slices, ready to be fried.

This is the breakfast I recall from weekends and school holidays, and a memory so important that, in my teens, with the guidance of Chris, I started to cure and smoke bacon of my own. It was the beginning of a fascination with cured meats that led eventually to what I do now – making charcuterie using pigs born and raised on the farm.

1 x pork belly, about 5cm thick

For the cure

800g sea salt

200g sugar

5g juniper berries

2.5g peppercorns

2g dried rosemary

1.5g dried thyme

1g dried bay leaf

Calculate 30g cure for each kilogram of meat.

Rub the weighed pork all over with the cure, being as thorough as you can. Place in a sealable container and put in the fridge for two weeks. Turn it over a few times during the curing process, massaging in the salt so that it penetrates.

When the two weeks are over, rinse off the cure and hang on a hook in the fridge to dry. Cut the unsmoked rashers for frying. If you have a cold smoker, smoke the bacon with a mixture of oak and beech, ensuring there is enough airflow in the smoking chamber to keep the smoke subtle and sweet.

Fingal Ferguson is a butcher, farmer, cheesemaker and maker of knives

Ching He Huang

AVO RYE, SUNNY CRISPY EGGS WITH A DRIZZLE OF SOY

It is 1984. I'm five years old. We have left my grandmother's farm in Taiwan for another farm in a foreign land and a family who speak a language we don't understand. They feed us strange food: dried bits of tough meat (biltong) served with a sort of cornmeal congee (*miele pap*) and wobbly things in plastic pots that my mother complains tastes of "off" milk (yoghurt). Everything smells different. We are a million miles from home and my grandparents, my Ah Kung and Ah Ma.

It has only been 24 hours, but already I miss the aroma of oranges on their farm, chasing chickens around their farmyard and the comforting rustling of bamboo trees in the wind. Who is this strange man (Uncle Robert)? Why are we now living on his land? And why is his wife (Aunty Susan) feeding us plants with a seed inside that they smash on bread (avocado)?

My brother and I enrol in the local school. We stick out like a sore thumb, dark haired and "different". People look at us like we don't belong – and we don't. We are in apartheid South Africa, the only ethnic "Chinese" children in a school of 500.

The first year is rough, but we learn to toughen up. We fight to make other children see who we are – human beings, just like them. We just want to fit in and play together.

Over time, we find friends, break bread and biltong together. I exchange Mum's tasty "Taiwanese-style railway bento" packed lunches for minced beef sandwiches with the kids at school. They love Chinese food.

One morning, mum makes us all avocados on toast, which she serves with a fried egg drizzled with soy sauce. As we eat, we watch as mum also tucks in and we all laugh. For the first time, we let go of our anxieties about living in a foreign land and the future looks bright – as bright as the sunny-side egg sitting on the avocado toast.

To this day, mum loves her avocados and will often ask if I have eaten them lately. For me, they are tied to that first memory of our family feeling positive about settling in South Africa. We found our way and created a home there, making the best of being East in the West.

We left for the UK in 1989. But during those turbulent apartheid times, food was our language – the language of connection, hope, friendship and love.

SERVES 1

1 tbsp rapeseed oil

2 large eggs

2 slices of seeded rye bread

1 ripe avocado, stone removed, flesh scooped out with a spoon

drizzle of light soy sauce

pinch of ground black pepper

pinch of dried chilli flakes

Heat a wok over a medium heat until it starts to smoke, then add the rapeseed oil. Crack the eggs into the wok and cook for 2 minutes or to your liking (I like mine crispy underneath and still a bit runny on top). Meanwhile, place the bread in the toaster and toast for 1 minute.

To serve, place the toast on a plate and spread with the avocado flesh. Place the eggs on top and drizzle over the soy sauce, then season with ground black pepper and eat immediately, accompanied by a cup of rooibos tea with a slice of lemon.

Ching He Huang MBE is a chef, broadcaster and food writer. Her books include Wok On, Asian Green *and* Stir Crazy

Jamie Oliver

PROPER PORRIDGE

One of my earliest recollections of comfort food is also one of my earliest memories, full stop. I was about five years old and I'd been dropped off with my sister, Anna, to stay at my nan and grandad's. They lived in a cute little bungalow, stuck to a budget and cooked every single day. Because me and Anna lived in a pub, there wasn't really a routine, but over at Nan and Grandad's, there was a real pattern to the day, starting at 7am sharp with Nan's ritual of proper porridge-making. There'd always be steaming cups of tea waiting for us on the table, and we'd climb into our chairs, feet swinging above the floor.

I can still picture the strange turquoise paper that lined the walls, the array of classic family photos on the mantelpiece, and the retro drinks cabinet. The radio – or the wireless as they called it – would always be on Radio 4 and we'd laugh as Grandad berated all the politicians during the news.

Nan's porridge was like nothing I'd ever tasted before. Having researched it, hers was a classic Scottish method and it was delicious.

It was at about this time that Ready Brek launched a brilliant ad campaign where a kid went to school glowing after tucking into a bowlful. Certainly, my nan's porridge gave me a glow – it was on another level.

SERVES 2

1 big builder's mug of coarse
     rolled large oats, such as
     Flahavan's

whole milk or cream, to serve

Some other ideas for serving porridge

Porridge can be a great way to pack in more of the good stuff when it comes to toppings – think fresh, stewed or roasted fruit, nuts and seeds. I like to lightly toast some sunflower, sesame and poppy seeds, crush them in a pestle and mortar with a pinch of ground cinnamon, mix them with some chopped dried fruit, then fold through. Or even take that combo, cook it fairly thick, pour it into an oiled tray about 2½cm thick, leave to set, cut into bars, and the next day, fry them in a little butter until golden and crispy on all sides, then serve with yoghurt and honey. Delicious.

Proper porridge should take around 18 minutes from start to finish. Pour the oats into a high-sided pan with 3 mugs of boiling water and a pinch of sea salt. It's important to start with water, as milk often scalds or boils over and doesn't smell or taste great when it does. Place the pan on a medium heat until it just starts to boil, then reduce to a simmer for 15 minutes, or until thick and creamy, stirring regularly, and adding a good splash of milk or cream towards the end to make it super-luxurious.

Nan would never be rushed when she made porridge, and all those torturous minutes later it would be poured into wide soup bowls and given to Grandad, Anna and me. We'd go to tuck in straight away, but Grandad always stopped us, so I'm going to stop you now. It's important to wait another 3 minutes for the residual chill of the bowl to slightly cool down the porridge from the outside in, so it remains soft, silky and oozy in the middle, but goes almost firm and jellified round the edges.

Grandad would always sprinkle his porridge with granulated brown sugar, and insist you waited a minute and a half for it to pull out the moisture from the porridge and turn into a bizarrely impressive caramelly glaze. I loved this, but couldn't help opting for a spoonful of golden syrup instead. What I found extraordinary was the way that over a couple of minutes, with a little jiggling of the bowl, the syrup always managed to creep down around and underneath the porridge, elevating it as if it were some sort of floating island.

We'd then marvel as Grandad got out a knife and cut the porridge into a chequerboard. He'd then pick up a jug of cold whole milk and gently pour it to one side of the bowl so it filled up every crack of the chequerboard like some crazy paddy-field drainage system. Then, and only then, were we given the signal to attack. And I have to say, that porridge was as good a breakfast as I've ever had.

Jamie Oliver OBE is a chef, broadcaster and campaigner

Nathan Outlaw

SMOKED HADDOCK & POTATO PANCAKES

Smoked haddock always reminds me of my grandad. He used to love what he called "finny haddock" – bright yellow stuff that came sealed in a plastic wrapper with a rosette of butter on top. I thought it was gross, mostly because it made the house smell for days after.

As a boy, I would go to Hastings old town where fish straight from the boats was sold out of rickety old shops. It was a fascinating way to spend a Sunday afternoon and the beginning of my love of fish, mostly due to curiosity about how different the species were. It was also the first place I saw haddock smoked properly rather than dyed bright yellow. The simple recipe below can be used for almost any meal; if you don't have time to make the pancakes, just do the haddock and serve it with toast. Or add a poached egg to make it more substantial.

SERVES 4

4 smoked haddock portions,
    about 120g each, skinned

1 litre whole milk

2 bay leaves

pinch of salt

Potato pancakes

100g plain flour

2 tsp baking powder

300g cold mashed potatoes

150ml full fat yoghurt

2 large free-range eggs, plus 1
    extra yolk

2 tbsp chopped tarragon

olive oil for cooking

Mustard crème fraîche

300g crème fraîche

1 tbsp wholegrain mustard

sea salt and freshly ground
    black pepper

Start with the batter for the potato pancakes. Sift the flour and baking powder into a bowl then mix in the mashed potato until thoroughly combined. In a separate bowl, whisk together the yoghurt, eggs and extra yolk then mix in the tarragon. Pour into the potato mixture and whisk until smooth. Set aside.

For the haddock, pour the milk into a large pan. Add the bay leaves and a good pinch of salt, bring to a simmer and remove from the heat. Leave to stand and infuse.

Cook the pancakes in batches. Heat a non-stick frying pan and add a drizzle of olive oil. Once hot, spoon in the batter a tablespoonful at a time, leaving room between them. Cook for 1 minute until golden on the underside then turn and cook for another 1-2 minutes. Pile onto a warmed plate and keep warm.

When all the pancakes are cooked, carefully place the haddock into the infused milk and slowly bring back to a simmer. Poach gently for 3 minutes.

Meanwhile, in a bowl, mix the crème fraîche and mustard and season to taste with salt and pepper. To serve, carefully lift the haddock out of the milk and drain on kitchen paper. Divide the pancakes between four warmed plates and add the fish. Serve the mustard crème fraîche on the side.

Nathan Outlaw is the chef-owner of Restaurant Nathan Outlaw, Port Isaac, Cornwall

Ping Coombes

HAKKA NOODLES

My hometown of Ipoh in Malaysia wasn't very big and the journey to school was short. I could stay in bed until half an hour before school started and be up and dressed in less than 10 minutes, the time it took my mum to prepare this noodle dish for breakfast.

We would dash to the car and my mum would hand over the plate of steaming noodles, complete with chopsticks, then drive like a bat out of hell while I tried not to drop noodles down my uniform. I became an expert at wolfing down my breakfast in a speeding car as it wove through traffic. I arrived at school stinking of garlic.

Of all the things my mum cooked, this was one of my favourites. Sometimes, when I didn't get up on time, she would pack the noodles into a container so I could have them later, but they were so enticing, I found it hard to wait. I once snuck off from assembly with a friend just so I could eat them. We were caught by the headmistress mid-slurp.

Now that I am a mum, I often cook this for my daughters, though I haven't yet made them eat it in a speeding car. It is very versatile and the pork mix keeps well in the fridge. It is easy to make and extremely flavourful. I often eat it for breakfast, though I can honestly eat it any time of day.

SERVES 4

For the pork and marinade

500g minced pork

1½ tbsp cornflour

1 tbsp oyster sauce

2 tbsp soy sauce

½ tsp sugar

¼ tsp white pepper

For the garlic oil

4 fat cloves of garlic, chopped as finely and evenly as possible

4 tbsp vegetable or other flavourless oil

For the pork sauce

1 tbsp oil

2 cloves of garlic, finely chopped

2 tbsp fish sauce

2 tbsp kecap manis (sweet soy sauce)

½ tsp sugar

250ml water

1½ tbsp cornflour diluted in 2 tbsp of cold water

40g coriander, chopped, stalks and all

For the noodles

4 bundles of wonton noodles or egg noodles

2 tbsp garlic oil

2 tbsp sweet soy sauce

2 tbsp oyster sauce

Mix the pork with the marinade ingredients and leave to stand at room temperature for at least 15 minutes.

Meanwhile, make the garlic oil. Heat the oil in a pan over a medium heat for about 1 minute, then drop in the chopped garlic. Swirl the pan, so the garlic is evenly distributed. As soon as it turns light gold, remove from the heat and set aside. The garlic will continue to cook and turn a rich golden colour. This can be made 1-2 days in advance and kept at room temperature.

To make the pork, heat the oil in a wok or frying pan over a medium heat. Add the garlic and fry until fragrant. Tip in the pork and gently fry until the pinkness is gone, then break into little pieces.

Add the fish sauce, kecap manis and sugar along with water. Bring to the boil, then lower the heat and simmer gently for 5 minutes. Don't worry if it seems like there is too much water.

Add the cornflour mixture to the pork and bring to the boil. As it cooks, the sauce will thicken and coat the pork. At this stage, add the coriander, fold in and turn off the heat.

To serve, cook the egg or wonton noodles. Drain well and coat with a couple of tablespoons of garlic oil. Season with sweet soy sauce and oyster sauce. Top with a generous dollop of pork mixture.

To eat, mix together and slurp loudly.

Ping Coombes is a former winner of Masterchef *and author of the cookbook* Malaysia: Recipes from a Family Kitchen

Jane Hodson

SOFT-BOILED EGGS WITH BUTTERY CUMIN SOLDIERS

All is well with the world when you have a chicken by your side. Time slows down and a quiet peacefulness prevails. They're affectionate, these curious creatures, and if you sit still enough they'll come up to you, keep you company, lean up against you as they soak up the sun.

Chickens featured prominently in my formative years. My parents always kept a few and these hens also became my friends. Even to this day, the soft sound of chicken talk, like the slow creaking of an old wooden gate on part-oiled hinges, is one of the most soothing sounds I know. Like all creatures, they have their individual personalities and I knew each one by name. Dolly was a silkie bantam who took to riding about the place on my shoulder. She was rather superior to the others of her kind and seemed somewhat resentful at being put back down onto the same earth as them. She acted as my sentinel, observant and mildly chatty. I knew well the soft reptile skin of her eyelids as she blinked her coal-black eyes at me.

Most of all, I remember the day the magic happened. I must have been about six years old and as I picked up one of the hens to cradle her in my arms, she laid her egg... directly into my hand. I can still recall the wonder of that moment; my small hand, outstretched before my eyes and holding onto that egg, tight enough not to drop it, yet gentle enough not to break it either. And as I looked closer, I saw that my fingers had created imprints in the shell. That was how I learnt that egg shells arrive soft into the world and only harden once in contact with the air.

That egg is the single most memorable egg that I have ever eaten (and I've munched my way through a fair few). I kept it with me all day long and that night I had it for my supper, soft boiled with lavishly buttered soldiers.

In those days, we had eggs for supper pretty much every night. We learnt how to sprinkle a pinch of salt into the opening at the top of the egg. It tasted good, but in reality, what you really got was a teaspoonful of salt as your first mouthful and then all the salt was gone. Years later it occurred to me to season the toast instead, to ensure a good meld of flavours in every bite. To this day, I can think of no other dish more reliably delicious or more joyous and comforting.

SERVES 1

2 eggs, at room temperature

2 slices of nutty or seeded bread

good farmhouse butter,
    at room temperature,
    for spreading

pinch of Maldon sea salt

freshly ground pepper

pinch of ground cumin

Fill a pan with water, deep enough for the eggs to be submerged when they're in it. Add a generous pinch of salt, which will stop the whites spreading too much, should the shell crack. Place on a hot stove.

Once the water is boiling, with a large spoon carefully lower in the eggs and set the heat at a gently rolling boil. Set a timer for 3-4 minutes (more or less, depending on the size of the egg).

Meanwhile, toast the bread and while still hot, slather with generous butter. Sprinkle over the sea salt and cumin with a good cracking of pepper. Cut into finger-sized strips, then take the eggs out of the pan and pop them into an egg cup. Cut off the lid, grab a soldier and tuck in.

The key to lifting this humble dish into the realms of the sublime is to pimp the soldiers. Let your imagination run free with this one. Instead of cumin, try spreading a lick of 'nduja onto the toast, smoosh on a couple of anchovies, or perhaps rub it over with a truffle, if you have one. Delicious flavour pairings with eggs are almost endless.

Jane Hodson is a private chef and former photojournalist. She cooks for clients in Somerset and around the world

Clerkenwell Boy

CHEESE AND MARMITE BABKA

The first time I remember eating Vegemite was at nursery school, where they'd make either Vegemite or peanut butter sandwiches for us while we were waiting to be picked up by our parents. They'd be cut into little fingers, which seemed really important to me at the time. Just like Marmite, it's a love or hate kind of thing and I fell in love with Vegemite immediately. Every breakfast, I'd always be the savoury kid. My mum would make me Vegemite and cheese on toast, while my sister tucked into jam and peanut butter. The last time I had some? This morning on toast, with loads of butter.

This recipe is the result of a collaboration with Mark Jankel from Shuk, a Middle Eastern restaurant in London that specialises in babkas. Traditionally, these enriched brioche dough pastries are sweet, but I decided to bring in my childhood favourite and make a Vegemite one instead. Although, in this instance we used Marmite, for two reasons: first, it's more readily available in the UK and, second, it actually spreads easier. Marmite has more of the consistency of honey, which means that for this recipe, it works best. To be honest, I love them both.

If you'd like to make a more traditional sweet babka, follow this recipe but use your own choice of fillings – below are some variations for you to try, but I suggest thinking of your favourite flavours and letting your imagination go wild!

SWEET VARIATIONS:

honey, apple & cinnamon

Nutella with toasted hazelnuts,
   or crunchy biscuits

cherry jam & pistachio

SAVOURY VARIATIONS:

Chorizo & Manchego

'Nduja & Parmesan

sun-dried tomatoes, mozzarella
   & olives

Dissolve the fresh yeast in the tepid water, then add the bread flour and plain flour to a mixer with a dough hook. Add the sugar and salt and mix well.

Add the whole egg and water-and-yeast mixture and mix until mostly incorporated.

Add the diced butter and mix on a medium setting until you have a smooth dough. This will take about 10 minutes. Put the dough in a bowl and allow to prove for one hour at room temperature.

Move to the fridge and leave overnight to continue to prove. Make the babka the following day – it is best to use the dough straight from the fridge.

For the béchamel, melt the butter on a medium heat, add the flour and cook stirring for about five minutes. Add the milk and whisk until smooth.

Cook for 10 minutes, then add the mustard, salt and grated Cheddar and mix until totally incorporated. Cover with clingfilm and allow to cool completely before using.

For the dough

9g fresh yeast

60g tepid water

150g bread flour

150g plain flour

60g caster sugar

90g whole egg

4g salt

30g butter, diced

For the béchamel

20g butter

20g plain flour

200g milk

6g Dijon mustard

2g salt

30g mature Cheddar cheese

For the savoury crumble

70g butter

60g flour

70g oats

2g smoked paprika

For the crumble, mix all the ingredients with a paddle attachment until they form a crumble. Cook on a tray in an even 1cm layer for 20 minutes at 150C/130C Fan/Gas 2.

If it starts to colour, open the oven and turn down the heat, then continue cooking for 20 minutes. Take out and allow to cool completely before using.

To assemble the babka, dust the worktop with plain flour and roll 480g of the dough into a big rectangle about 3mm thick. Spread 220g of béchamel over the whole surface of the dough (leave 1 cm free on each edge). Spread an even layer of 100g grated Cheddar and 140g savoury crumble on top of the béchamel. Dot 40g of Marmite with a teaspoon over the surface of the savoury crumble.

Starting from the side closest to you, roll up the pastry (like a Swiss roll), keeping it quite tight.

Check the video highlight on @shuklondon Instagram to see the next bit – cut the roll lengthways and separate the two pieces – cross over on one end and twist. Then twist all the way along to the other end. Place in a pre-greased loaf tin. Let it prove in a warm place for two hours until it starts to swell and become puffy.

Lightly brush the surface of the babka with egg wash.

Set the oven to 190C/170C Fan/Gas 5 and cook the babka for 30-35 mins.

Clerkenwell Boy is a food and travel Instagrammer whose books include The Cook for Syria Recipe Book

Nibbly
Bits

Stanley Tucci

POTATO CROQUETTES

When I was 12, we lived in Italy for a year and at one point I had stomach flu and was laid up in bed for a few days. Obviously, during that time, I ate very little, because I had no interest in eating. But as I started to feel better and became more and more hungry, I craved only one thing – these potato croquettes. I don't know why, but I couldn't stop thinking about them. When I was finally healthy enough to get to the kitchen, I asked my mother if she would make some for me – and, being a great mother, she did. I devoured them. These little savoury treats are still one of my favourite recipes and, whether you are recovering from stomach flu or in perfect health, I promise you will find them delicious. They are also very simple to make and can be served as an appetiser, a side dish or just something to snack on. They are a moreish comfort food for me and will be for you as well. Enjoy.

SERVES 6

4 medium-sized floury potatoes, peeled and quartered

2 large eggs, beaten

50g plain dried breadcrumbs

2 tbsp plain flour

3 tbsp finely grated Pecorino Romano cheese

1 tbsp chopped flat-leaf parsley

sea salt

60ml olive oil, plus more as needed

Place the potatoes in a large saucepan and fill with enough water to cover. Bring to a boil and cook until they are tender when pierced with a fork, about 15-20 minutes.

Drain the potatoes and mash them in a bowl with a potato masher. Add the eggs, breadcrumbs, flour, cheese, parsley and salt to taste. Mix them with your hands to make a firm, dry mixture, adding more breadcrumbs or flour as necessary.

Heat the olive oil in a small frying pan (about 20cm in diameter) set over a medium heat. Roll tablespoons of the dough between the palms of your hands to form logs 4-5cm long. When the oil is hot but not smoking, add a few croquettes to the pan and fry until lightly browned on all sides, about 6 minutes.

Transfer the cooked croquettes to a plate lined with paper towels to drain before serving. Continue to cook the croquettes in small batches. Add more oil to the pan if necessary, being sure to allow it to heat up before adding the croquettes. The croquettes are best served immediately, but they can be made ahead of time and reheated in the oven if necessary.

Stanley Tucci is an actor, filmmaker and cookbook author; his most recent book is Taste: My Life in Food

Richard Corrigan

SODA BREAD

Growing up, the house was always filled with the smell of freshly baked bread. Truly, it was the smell of my childhood. My mother had a near obsession with baking bread – there would always be three loaves in the kitchen at any one time. From a toddler to my teens she'd get me kneading the bread and this is where my own love affair with the stuff started. I remember holding the loaves to my ear and giving them a little tap to hear that hollow sound – which lets you know the bread is perfectly cooked. It's such a vivid memory of fond times.

So this is my mother's soda bread recipe, a staple that I had every day growing up in Ireland. It has the addition of a little organic honey and treacle, which deepens the flavour and sweetens it up slightly, making it the perfect match for smoked food, shellfish and cheese. It's best eaten on the day it's baked but if you have any left over (not a common occurrence in my home), toast it before topping with lashings of good quality salted butter and cured meats. Another tip is to put a damp cloth over the bread after it has come out of the oven.

This helps to keep as much moisture as possible inside as the bread cools down. The best flour is stone ground and comes from Shipton Mill in Gloucestershire. It has a low gluten content and I highly recommend trying to get your hands on some if you can. It's what we use every morning when we make our daily loaves at Bentley's. For an afternoon treat, add more honey and some currants to this recipe to get a sort of curney loaf. It's incredible with just butter or blue cheese.

MAKES 1 LARGE LOAF

250g plain flour
10g salt
15g bicarbonate of soda
150g wholemeal flour
150g jumbo oat flakes
1 tbsp clear honey
1 tbsp black treacle
500ml buttermilk

Preheat the oven to 200C/180C Fan/Gas 6 and line a baking sheet with greaseproof paper.

Combine all of the dry ingredients together in a bowl. Make a well in the centre, then mix in the honey, treacle and buttermilk, working everything together lightly with your hands until you have a loose, wet dough.

Flour your hands and shape the dough into a round and lift it onto the lined baking sheet. Cut a cross in the top (to help separate it into quarters when it cooks). Transfer to the oven and bake for about 45 minutes or until the loaf sounds hollow when you tap the base with your knuckles.

Transfer to a wire rack, cover with a damp cloth and leave to cool. Don't even think of putting dairy spread on it. This bread needs and deserves butter.

Richard Corrigan is chef-patron of restaurants including Corrigan's and Bentley's in London, The Park Café in Dublin, and Virginia Park Lodge in County Cavan, and the author of The Clatter of Forks and Spoons

Felicity Cloake

MUSHY PEA FRITTERS

Despite being born and brought up entirely in Britain, I somehow managed to avoid our "national dish" until well into my teenage years. Then, at the age of 17, I acquired a northern boyfriend. Horrified at the gaping hole in my education, he marched me straight off to Bizzie Lizzie's chippie in Skipton to ease me in gently with a fishcake (a Yorkshire fishcake, I discovered, bears little resemblance to the things sold down south under that name) and chips, served with buttered sliced white and a pot of tea.

Several things perplexed me as we waited, sweating slightly in the beef-fat fug – why would you drink hot tea with hot food in a hot restaurant? Who eats bread with a plate of potatoes? What on earth was dandelion and burdock? – but chief among them was my love's reaction when I suggested that some sauce might be a nice accompaniment. Tangy tartare maybe, I said, considering the sea of beige food in front of me, or the peppery watercress my mum sometimes did with salmon.

To his credit, he didn't throw me straight into the Leeds and Liverpool Canal as I certainly deserved. Instead, sighing deeply, he pointed at the bottle of malt vinegar. That, apparently, was all the sauce I needed.

Reader, annoyingly, it turned out he was right. Having more than made up for lost time in the fish and chip department since, I've come to appreciate this soothing uniformity of flavour, a quality shared by many traditional British foodstuffs (see also potato pie, porridge and suet puddings), and, in its way, as pleasurable as any bold spicing or zingy freshness. In an often noisy world, sometimes quiet is just fine.

They don't serve these mushy pea fritters at Bizzie Lizzie's – they're something I came across at the Star of the Sea chippie in Broadstairs – but for those who don't eat fish, or indeed those who prefer everything on their plate to be deep fried, they're a great partner for a bag of chips. Tea and bread, optional – but hold the sauce, please.

Dried marrowfat peas are found in health food shops, or easily bought online; if you happen to have a piece of ham, gammon or bacon, you can add this to the pan with the peas, or cook them in stock if you prefer. You could even add herbs or spices if you must, but personally I wouldn't. A cooking thermometer is very useful here.

MAKES 6 FRITTERS

250g dried marrowfat peas

½ carrot

½ onion or shallot

knob of butter

For the batter

200g plain flour

¼ tsp salt

⅛ tsp baking powder

250ml cold beer or fizzy water

fat, to fry

Soak the peas overnight in cold water, then drain. Put in a pan, cut the carrot in two and add to the pan along with the onion. Cover with roughly 5cm cold water and bring to the boil, then turn down the heat and cook until the peas are soft enough to mash, adding more water if necessary.

Remove and discard the carrot and onion and roughly mash the peas, keeping about half whole. The finished texture should be a bit like porridge – thick, but still liquid, so keep cooking, or indeed add more water if needed. Stir in a knob of butter or other fat, and season to taste. To make things easier, use a tin of mushy peas instead, drained of excess liquid.

Allow to cool to room temperature and then, using lightly floured hands if necessary, form into six balls and flatten. Put in the fridge for at least an hour, until firm.

When you're ready to cook, put the flour in the freezer, then heat the fat in a fryer, or fill a deep, heavy-based pan no more than a third full – I like to cook these in beef dripping or good lard, but sunflower or groundnut oil will do. Use a thermometer to tell when it reaches about 185C (if you don't have one, a cube of bread should turn golden in 15 seconds).

While the fat is heating, whisk the salt and baking powder into the cold flour, then pour in the beer until you have a thickish batter. Working quickly, dip two of the patties in batter, shake off the excess and lower into the oil. Fry for about 4-6 minutes until golden, turning occasionally.

Lift on to a slotted rack to drain, sprinkle with salt and serve immediately or keep warm in a low oven while you repeat.

Felicity Cloake writes about food for many outlets, including The Guardian. *Her books include* Completely Perfect *and* Red Sauce, Brown Sauce

Niki Segnit

FRENCH TOAST WITH FRESH BROWN SAUCE

How many meals did my dad cook in the 18 years that I lived with my parents? One, in the cramped kitchen of a rented cottage near Land's End. We went there most summer holidays. The sight of my father standing barefoot at the Belling stove, in an apron, pushing a fish slice around a frying pan, was quite a novelty. For us both.

My memories of those Cornish summers primarily concern food, not that any of it was fancy, or even notably better than the food I ate at home (my mother was and is an excellent cook). It was just that the happiness of those holidays has preserved what I ate in the aspic of particularity. Crabs plucked from a tank in a remote fishing village. Peppery Cornish pasties from a bakery at the end of a sickening hairpin car ride. If someone had told us there was a good fish and chip shop you had to crawl three miles over jagged stones to get to, we'd have given it a go. We were the first family addicted to inconvenience food.

Dad's dish was French toast, a favourite of his from childhood. Egg and bread: for so simple a meal, it's remarkable how different-tasting its many iterations are. Poached egg on grainy wholewheat. Soft-boiled eggs with buttered soldiers. Egg mayo on rye, scrambled eggs in a poppy-seed bagel. What I instantly loved about French toast was its crisp surface, almost like a skin. If you like your fried eggs with a lacy brown perimeter, French toast is that all over, the char of the surface set off by the sweet sponginess within. Dad had a hit.

It would be neat to say that my father, likewise, under his crisp exterior, was soft and sweet inside. Neat, but untrue. My dad was tough on the inside too – which was probably the reason he didn't cook. Times have changed. When we visit him now, he's nearly always in the kitchen, trying out a recipe. He even has his own apron.

There are many variations on French toast, some including vanilla or cinnamon. My children like these sweet versions with berries or a compote on the side. I prefer to let the egginess speak for itself, accompanied by a sauce whose boldness reminds me of my father.

For the sauce

100g dates without stones

75g fresh tomatoes

1 tbsp maple syrup

2 tsp sherry vinegar

pinches of ground allspice,
    cumin and salt

For the toast

2 large eggs

2 tbsp milk

pinch of salt

4 slices of white bread

2 tsp vegetable oil

For the sauce, blend all of the ingredients in a small food processor. I like to keep it a little coarse. If you can make it the day before, do. It'll taste better.

For the toast, warm the oil in the pan over a medium heat. Beat the eggs with the milk and salt for a few seconds. Pour about a quarter of the egg-milk mixture onto a flat plate. Lay a slice of bread in the mixture and let it soak for about 15 seconds, before turning the slice over and leaving for another 15 seconds. The bread should be nice and coated. Fry it in the hot oil for about 30 seconds, until mottled brown, then flip and allow to colour on the other side. Repeat for the other three slices. Serve with a dollop of the sauce.

Niki Segnit is a food writer and author of The Flavour Thesaurus *and* Lateral Cooking

Kate Trelawny

NAM JIM

I don't really have food memories from when I was young. I was plagued with eating disorders, which made food the ultimate enemy and something I found no pleasure in. It stayed that way throughout my youth until, in a pivotal moment up a hillside in Thailand, my life was changed forever.

In a blinding flash, it dawned on me that, far from being the enemy, food was in fact something glorious and beautiful, boundless in its magnificence. Nature's palette, if you like. I suddenly appreciated that cashews grow on trees, that lemongrass springs from the ground, that all this wonderful produce could be delicious and life-giving. I realised that food was an art form, something to be embraced in all its varied wonder. In just 20 minutes, I had not only changed my views on food, but reset the course of my life.

Thirty years later, food is my greatest passion. It's what I do and it's what I think about. What makes me most happy is ease – keeping it simple, yet packing a massive punch. I love having a secret concoction to hand that will transform simple ingredients into something special. This nam jim sauce is one of them. It, too, is a legacy of that trip to Thailand. It didn't just change my awareness of the world and how to live in it, it gave me an invaluable lesson in sweet, sour, salt and spice.

MAKES A 350ML JAR

6 limes, juiced

100g caster sugar

1 tbsp fish sauce (optional)

bunch mint leaves

bunch coriander, stalks included

1 tbsp soy sauce

2 green chillies

Put the whole lot in a blender and blitz. Adjust the salt, sugar and/or chilli to your taste.

This goes with all meats, fish, salads, vegetables, even cheese. It will keep in the fridge for at least 3 weeks, but it is so moreish that I doubt it will last that long.

Kate Trelawny is a private chef, based in London. She cooks for clients from the worlds of fashion, music and beyond

Jacob Kenedy

BOILED ARTICHOKES

My earliest clear memory is of sitting on my grandpa Joh's lap, pretending to be pirates as he shared an artichoke with me. He died of cancer when I was about two, to which he had already lost an eye. With his eyepatch, he made a convincing pirate.

We were sitting on the chair closest to the window onto the garden of his home on Glebe Place in Chelsea, which would become the garden I grew up in. I remember him pulling off the leaves of a slightly warm boiled globe artichoke, dipping them in lemony butter and putting the tender part of one in my mouth, then the next in his. Then he carefully removed the choke from the heart and fed me the whole thing, butter-dipped bite by butter-dipped bite. I grew up with an irrational resentment of the doctors I had never met, who took his eye and didn't spot that the cancer had metastasised until it was too late.

Now this says a lot – mostly about the nature of memory. There is little chance I can remember such detail from the age of two and the story must have grown in the retelling, as my mum told it to me and I told it to others. But it also says a lot about generosity, a lot about my grandpa and a lot about artichokes.

I love artichokes. I love them raw or fried or braised or mashed or in pasta or with meat or with fish or on their own. But I especially love them boiled. It is a rare treat to find a restaurant that will humble itself by doing them (tip: try Nepenthe in Big Sur, or the Giant Artichoke in Geyserville, both in California). I eat them this way with my mum, maybe every fortnight. This way, we remember.

This dish is best with globe artichokes – the really big, tough-leafed ones from California – none of that tender-fleshed so-good-you-can-eat-it-raw nonsense from Italy. But you can boil any artichokes this way and they will be good.

SERVES AS MANY AS
YOUR PAN WILL TAKE

artichokes (any sort, but
preferably globe – you need
one huge globe per person
as a very satisfying starter, or
indeed a very light meal)

lemons

peppercorns

cloves

bay leaves

garlic, optional

salt

butter

You can leave the stalks on the artichokes, or snap them off at the base of the bud. In either case, you should trim the brown cut base from the stalk and cook it with the artichoke – it has a tough outside, but a delicious centre.

Put the artichokes in a big pot. For each artichoke, add a slice of lemon, a few peppercorns, a clove or two, a bay leaf and if you like, a whole clove of garlic. Cover with cold water and add a good amount of salt (for a big saucepan, a small handful – the water needs to be salty enough to season the artichokes).

Weigh the artichokes down with a couple of plates that just fit inside the pot, and set it over a high heat. Once it boils, reduce the heat. Big globe artichokes will need a good hour and a half to boil this way, smaller varieties will take less time. It is important they are fully cooked through. Otherwise, they won't be tender, the choke will stick to the heart, and as they cool they will blacken and turn bitter inside. To tell if they are cooked through, poke a skewer into the base – it should feel tender inside. If there is resistance in the middle, cook them longer.

Once cooked, lift the artichokes from the water and set them upside down to drain. I like to let them cool for maybe 20 minutes before eating, so they are warm rather than hot – but often I don't have the patience.

While they are resting, melt a lot of butter (50g per person, perhaps) with lemon juice (maybe half a lemon per head) and a little salt.

To eat the artichokes, pull off the leaves one by one, dip the tender base in the lemon butter, then use your teeth to suck-pull the flesh from the leaf. This is slow eating – and excellent for conversation. When you get to the prickly purple leaves in the middle, discard them, and pull the choke (bristles) off the heart (cup-shaped base). The heart is the trophy: dip it in butter and enjoy.

Any leftover artichokes can be refrigerated and eaten cold, the same way, but with really good extra virgin olive oil and vinegar, instead of butter and lemon.

Jacob Kenedy is a chef and co-founder of Bocca di Lupo restaurant and Gelupo, all in London

Sally Clarke

MARINATED FRESH ANCHOVIES

My love of food and farmers' markets was triggered on family holidays in France during the 1960s with my parents and two brothers. The older we got, the further south we would travel each summer, singing together along the D roads in our Rover 100.

En route, we would choose our picnic lunches from village traiteurs, boulangeries and street markets – pâtés, cheeses and baguettes, buttery fruit tarts, peaches and *fraises des bois*.

Then, once we reached our destination (usually a modest family-run restaurant with rooms, close to the sea), we would start exploring, not only the rock pools and ice-cream shops, but also the menus. We always found something different to taste – artichokes, courgettes and weirdly-shaped tomatoes, huge bowls of mussels, calf's brain…

I am not sure when or where I ate my first raw anchovy – could it have been then, in Brittany, sitting by a fishing port in the sunshine? Or was it much later, in California, at the wonderful Zuni restaurant in San Francisco? Here, anchovy fillets are often served as a pre-starter, drizzled with olive oil and a scattering of finely sliced celery.

Wherever it was, I still love them – and although, to the uninitiated, the thought of any anchovy, let alone a raw one, is something to be scared of, I am a keen persuader and would love to think that this simple method of preparation could help convert a few antis. Use this recipe only when the freshest of anchovies are available to you. They should be firm to the touch, with glistening eyes and scales, and should have a fresh, appealing smell of the sea.

SERVES 4

12 fresh anchovies

2 lemons

olive oil

celery sticks from the heart,
  including leaves

black pepper

Rinse the anchovies under a cold running tap, gently rubbing away the scales. Make a small incision in the belly and remove the innards. Rinse again under cold running water.

Dry the fish with kitchen paper and lay them on a chopping board. With a small knife, slide the blade over the backbone, from the head to the tail, removing the fillet from the bone with one easy stroke. Turn the fish over and repeat on the other side. Once they are all filleted, wipe them gently with kitchen paper and check that there are no bones.

Lay the fillets like soldiers on a flat serving dish, silver skin side up, and sprinkle with the juice of 1 lemon. Cover and chill in the fridge for at least 20 minutes.

Slice the celery on the angle, including the leaves.

Remove the dish from the fridge, drizzle the fillets with a little olive oil and some ground pepper, and scatter with the sliced celery.

Cut the remaining lemon into 8 wedges and place around the dish.

Serve chilled, with bread and butter or sourdough toasts, radishes, olives and a lovely glass of rosé.

Sally Clarke is a chef and founder of Sally Clarke restaurant, bakery and shop in London

Mitch Tonks

SHRIMPS ON TOAST

As a small boy, I lived in Weston-super-Mare with my grandmother, who was a cook of necessity. A few hundred yards down the road, across the stream where I used to catch minnows and sticklebacks, were the local shops and I was often dispatched with a note to the Good Cheers Cellars to buy my nan's Woodpecker cider and Player's No 10.

There was a Mac Fisheries fishmonger, too. I would peer through the window outside, standing on tiptoes to see what was on the counter. There were piles of shrimps, crabs galore and fish that, at the time, I didn't recognise, all of it simply laid out. I can still smell it – not a fishy smell, more shellfishy, like cooked crabs and the smell of ozone.

Brown shrimps, a rarity now, were a staple for us back then. When I got home, nan and I would sit and peel them at her dark wooden table, which had a leaf that could be pulled out for Sunday lunch. She would do a trick with the heads and legs – something about Adam and Eve. I never really understood – I still don't – but it always fascinated me to watch. Once the shrimps were peeled, we would make sandwiches – just ordinary white sliced, spread with butter and white pepper, then filled with handfuls of shrimps. Nan would have Sarson's vinegar on the table, though it was too sharp for me. We would cut the sandwiches into four and eat them. I can still taste the sweet, almost earthy flavour and feel the shrimps in my mouth. I would look around and see the movement of nan in the kitchen behind the fluted glass that separated dining from cooking. As she busied herself with the preparations for dinner, I was kept quiet with my sandwich and the contentment of home and of being with her.

These days, I buy ready-peeled shrimps and pot them with butter to spread on toast. There is always debate as to whether potted shrimps should be served warm or at room temperature. I like them both ways, though sometimes, as here, I just warm peeled shrimps in melted butter and pour them straight over thick toast.

SERVES 2

150g peeled brown shrimps

pinch of ground mace

75g butter

salt and white pepper

1 tbsp parsley, very finely chopped

lemon wedges for serving

thick bread, for toasting

First, toast the bread. Melt the butter in a saucepan, with a pinch of mace, salt and plenty of white pepper, then stir in the shrimps and allow to warm through for a minute or so. Add the parsley and spoon over the toast.

The dish can be spiced up a little by a sprinkling of cayenne pepper.

Mitch Tonks is a chef, author and broadcaster and owner of The Seahorse restaurant in Dartmouth and the Rockfish chain of takeway seafood restaurants

Henry Harris

CHICKEN LIVER PÂTÉ

Mum was – and still is – a serial entertainer. She always did things well, with proper structure. Nibbles and olives with drinks, a fish starter, a meat course, cheese – in the French way, before dessert – and a choice of three puddings, which always seemed to include grape brulée and a chocolate roulade, referred to in our house as "elephant's turd".

Summer lunches in the garden were populated with good things from the barbecue – grilled prawns, sausages, steaks and lamb chops – with the starters laid out on the table. There would be whole smoked mackerel with sweet mustard sauce, smoked salmon, homemade taramasalata, salami and prosciutto, and Mum's chicken liver pâté, served in its terrine with a knife plunged into it. It was a lovely, old-fashioned pâté, with plenty of garlic and a texture that could be squashed onto toast.

Dad would grill bread on the barbecue to go with it. In the 1960s, he had worked in the computer business, but at one of our summer lunches, he announced that he thought he could make better sausages than the ones he had just cooked. He found a butcher in Yorkshire who taught him how, then opened a sausage shop in Hove. That grew into a deli and wine shop, on the back of which he opened a restaurant in Brighton, called Le Grandgousier. It was unashamedly Gallic and the chicken liver pâté appeared on the menu every day for all of its 17 years.

I had thought when I was younger that I would be a barrister. But as I watched the restaurant grow, my thoughts of law turned to cooking. And so it was that, years later, when I opened my own restaurant, Racine, the chicken liver pâté made the same daily appearance.

1 kg trimmed chicken livers

500g Toulouse sausage meat,
    broken up

5 tbsp panko breadcrumbs

2 cloves garlic, crushed

1 tbsp herbes de Provence

7-8 generous turns of
    a peppermill

½ tbsp salt

1 tsp green peppercorns

125ml port

125ml white wine

5-6 rashers green streaky bacon

Preheat the oven to 150C/130C Fan/Gas 2.

Finely chop or coarsely mince the chicken livers, then add to a bowl with all the other ingredients, except the bacon, and mix together until thoroughly combined.

Press the mixture into a terrine (about 1.5 litre), and press the bacon rashers onto the top. Cover with tin foil.

Place the terrine in a deep roasting tin and pour boiling water around the outside until it comes about halfway up the side of the terrine. Place in the oven and cook for about 45 minutes-1 hour; the core temperature should be 67C. (Take care not to get a false probe reading from too close to the bottom of the terrine.)

Remove from the oven and the bain marie and leave to stand for 30 minutes. Cut a piece of wood or plastic to fit the top, wrap in parchment paper, then lay on top of the terrine. Weigh it down with full tins of tomatoes and place in the fridge until cold.

Serve with good bread and cornichons.

Henry Harris was one of the original head chefs of Bibendum, launched The Fifth Floor at Harvey Nichols and, in 2002, opened the acclaimed Racine as chef patron. He is now chef and co-owner of the Three Compasses pub and Bouchon Racine in Farringdon

Santiago Lastra

CRAB CHALUPA

I started cooking when I was 15, back home in Mexico in the town of Cuernavaca, just south of Mexico City. Until then, I'd always wanted to be an economist or mathematician – I was even on the regional school maths team. But one day, I found a recipe for crab dip on the back of a box of Ritz crackers in the supermarket. I bought the ingredients and went home to make it for my family. They loved it – so I bought an Italian recipe booklet and worked my way through that as well.

It made me wonder if maybe I might enjoy cooking for a living, so I found a part-time job in an Italian restaurant. I loved everything about it: the steam, the heat, the pressure, the smells and the passion. It filtered straight into my veins. Sixteen years later, I still feel the same way I did that very first time I put on an apron.

But a few months after I started at the restaurant, tragedy struck. My grandmother, grandfather and father all passed away within a month of each other. It was a devastating time for me and my family and, for a while, I stopped going to school. I decided to go back to the restaurant, however, and I remember coming home with fresh bread and wine and making pasta for my mother and brother. Suddenly, the sadness turned to happiness. It was then that I knew I wanted to dedicate my life to creating other moments like this: moments with the power to banish sadness, at least temporarily – the power to make people happy.

The recipe here is my interpretation of that supermarket crab dip, the first thing I ever cooked – and the only thing I ever got to make for my father.

SERVES 10

For the brown crab purée

330g brown crab meat

20g chipotle chilli

For the chalupa (you can use totopos or tostadas instead)

200g corn masa

oil, for frying

For the pistachio cream

50g pistachios

10g roasted garlic

50ml water

For the habanero salsa

18g Scotch bonnet or habanero chilli

15ml lime juice

100ml water

½ tsp salt

For the crab and enoki dressing

5g habanero salsa (see above)

20g chopped fermented gooseberries (you can use olives instead)

20ml lime juice

100g white crab meat

100g cooked enoki mushrooms

salt, for seasoning

Put the brown crab meat in a pan, bring to a simmer and cook until it starts to curdle and thicken. The water will evaporate and it will resemble wet scrambled eggs. Blend until smooth, then sieve. Blitz in the chipotle, season and put to one side.

For the chalupa, mix the corn masa with water until it is the consistency of Play-Doh – you'll need about 165ml water for 200g masa. Ensure the oil is at 170C and place a ladle inside to heat up. Press the masa, not too thin, in a tortilla press (or you can press the dough between two pans to make the disc). Lay over the back of the ladle to form a bowl shape and lightly press to fix into place. Lay the ladle gently into the oil and hold for a few seconds. Let go and the chalupa should release itself; but if not, lightly run a small palette knife underneath to ease it off.

Fry for a few more seconds. Once crisp, remove and place on a cooling rack.

For the pistachio cream, blend the pistachios with the water and roasted garlic, season and reserve.

To make the salsa and the dressing, simply combine the ingredients in a bowl.

To build the chalupas, spread some of the pistachio cream on top, then add the brown crab purée and finally the crab and enoki dressing. Eat with your hands!

Santiago Lastra is the chef and co-owner at London's KOL restaurant, which received its first Michelin star in 2022

Little Lunches

Rosie Ramsden

CRAB TOASTED SANDWICHES

It's August on the creek. We hop over long-burnt grass to the water's edge, nibbling salty stems of samphire on the way, and test the temperature with our toes. The creek smells of salt and iron and teabag, and swimmers hold their heads high for fear of swallowing the carpet-like seaweed. We squelch out through the grey-blue-black sludge until we are deep enough to swim.

Crawling back onto the bank with blackened toenails and green slime stuck to our ankles, we settle by the tree where a swing has been assembled by kids just like us. We climb the branches, swing a little, then plunge back into the river.

Finally, our energy spent, we drip our way back to sunhats and scratchy rugs, where the dry stems of broken reeds poke through the wool. And there, in three different Mackie's ice cream tubs, the promise of a hot chipolata and mum's famous coffee-chocolate brownies, crab sandwiches and a blue plastic beaker of warm Old Jamaica ginger beer.

SERVES 4

For the samphire

100g samphire

75ml water

75ml cider vinegar

75g sugar

For the crab

300g white crabmeat

2 tbsp brown crabmeat

½ tsp Dijon mustard

juice of ½ a lemon

2 tbsp crème fraîche

salt and lots of black pepper

4 slices good brown bread or
  sourdough

butter, to spread

Rinse the samphire in cold water and trim anything tough and woody. Heat the water, vinegar and sugar in a wide saucepan until the sugar has dissolved. Add the samphire to the pan and stir, making sure the samphire is under the pickle brine. Simmer for 1 minute then remove from the heat and allow to cool.

Mix the crab meat, mustard, Dijon, lemon juice and crème fraîche in a bowl. Crunch on some black pepper and season with salt.

Toast the bread, spread with butter, then top with the crab and pickled samphire.

Rosie Ramsden is a food stylist, recipe writer and artist

Anita Cheung

CANTONESE HEALING CHICKEN SOUP

My lasting memory of my mum in the kitchen when I was growing up is of her armed with a cleaver and a pair of Marigolds, her two essential tools. Although, like every Chinese family, we made dumplings together – it takes so much time that everyone has to get involved – she certainly didn't teach me how to cook. She did, though, teach me how to eat.

You could tell she got immense satisfaction from making food we enjoyed and, even though she worked almost every night, she always made sure we had a home-cooked dinner. This is where she poured her love: into the food she cooked. Often it was Cantonese-style, some of the ingredients flown from Hong Kong as you couldn't get hold of them in the UK back then – and certainly not on the Isle of Man, where we lived.

On her days off, we would go out to eat, sampling the finest food the Isle of Man had to offer. We always tried new things, savouring meals together and discussing whether it was good, bad, fresh or well balanced. Even today my inclination is to order something I've never tasted and, whenever I go home or mum visits, I always ask her to cook something new.

Food in our family has never been just about sustenance or the way things taste. Nowhere is medicine as integrated into the food we eat as in Chinese culture. You know that section in Chinese supermarkets with all the crazy dried... things? That's for the cook in every Chinese household who knows how to make home remedies for all sorts of ailments and maladies. In my house, that person was my mother. Like her mother before her, she knew which ingredients would cure certain illnesses. This hereditary knowledge, passed down from generation to generation, is testament to over two millennia of Traditional Chinese Medicine with food medicine at its core.

My mother always includes some kind of soup in a meal, as is traditional in Chinese culture. This one, passed down to me by her, helps lift and nourish the system. In traditional medicine, balance is everything. Every ingredient, herb or spice has specific properties – cold, hot, up, down, inward, outward – which combine to restore balance in a person's system, or promote health and wellbeing.

This soup uses Cantonese cooking techniques with a light touch, with added berries that emphasise and deepen the quality and flavour of each ingredient. It has a delicate kind of richness that tries to bring every ingredient used into The Ultimate Balance.

1 whole chicken (organic if
possible)

large knob of ginger, thinly
sliced

6 dried jujube/Chinese red dates

15-20 dried goji berries

15g dried longan kernels

15g Chinese yam/wai san

2 medium-large carrots, thickly
sliced

1½ tbsp fish sauce (or more to
taste, if required)

For the dip

3 large knobs of ginger, peeled
and grated

2 spring onions, chopped

salt

4 tbsp vegetable oil (such as
rapeseed or peanut)

Rinse the dried ingredients to remove dust and dirt, and soak for a few hours.

Place the chicken, minus its giblets, into a large pot with everything except the fish sauce and cover with water.

Bring to the boil, skim off the froth, then turn the heat to a gentle simmer and cook for 2 hours.

Make the ginger and spring onion dip. Put the ginger and spring onion in a heatproof bowl with 3 large pinches of salt and place in the sink ready for the hot oil. Heat the oil until smoking, then slowly and carefully pour it over the ginger and spring onion. Caution: the hot oil will spit once it touches the ginger and spring onion so make sure to protect your eyes and skin. Add more salt as required.

Remove the chicken and separate the meat to serve with the ginger and spring onion dip. Add fish sauce to the soup and simmer for a further 10 minutes. Serve the soup alongside the chicken, with some boiled rice and stir-fried greens to create a typical Cantonese family meal.

Anita Cheung is the founder of Bristol street-food stall Ah-Ma's Dumplings

Raymond Blanc

FRICASSÉE OF WILD MUSHROOMS

For my seventh birthday, my father gave me a beautiful hand-drawn treasure map. It detailed all the best places to go hunting and fishing in the area, including where to forage for the best mushrooms. I would return home with my treasure and, if I had gathered enough, Maman Blanc would cook this delicious fricassée. Nowadays, I am a lucky boy in that I have the luxury of my own valley of wild mushrooms within the gardens of Le Manoir aux Quat'Saisons.

The dish is simple to make, but it relies on the quality and freshness of the mushrooms. It has all the earthy flavours of the forest and lots of juice just waiting to be mopped up with a piece of crusty French bread. The best mushrooms, if you can get them, are girolles, pieds de mouton (hedgehog mushrooms), pieds bleus, chanterelles and oyster mushrooms – though, of course, all types of wild mushrooms can be used for this dish. You could also use herbs such as tarragon, coriander and chervil instead of parsley.

SERVES 4

40g butter, unsalted

30g shallot or white onion, chopped

1 clove garlic, peeled and crushed to a purée

400g mixed wild mushrooms (e.g. chanterelle, girolle, pieds bleus, button mushrooms)

5g black trumpet mushrooms

1 tbsp lemon juice

100ml dry white wine, boiled for 30 seconds

4 pinches sea salt

4 pinches freshly ground black pepper

small handful of flatleaf parsley, coarsely chopped

120g (2 whole) Roma tomatoes, quartered, deseeded and cut into 5mm dice

For the croutons

½ small baguette

1 peeled clove of garlic

For the croutons, cut the baguette into 20 slices, 3mm thick. Toast under the grill or lay out on an oven tray and cook in the oven at 180C/160C Fan/Gas 4 until lightly golden. Rub with the clove of garlic and put to one side.

Pick over the mushrooms, removing all twigs and leaves. Cut off the base of the root and divide the mushrooms into two or three pieces. If you are using pieds de moutons, scrape off their velvety hairs with a small knife. Put the black trumpets to one side.

Plunge the other mushrooms into 3 litres of water and quickly swirl them with your hands for no more than 10 seconds. Mushrooms are great sponges and will soak up the water very quickly, so ensure this process is done very swiftly. Lift them out onto a clean towel, pat dry and reserve.

Melt 20g butter in a large frying pan over a medium heat and soften the chopped shallots for 30 seconds, without colouring. The gentle heat will sweeten the shallots, remove the sulphur and transform the starch into sugar – into flavour. Turn the heat up high, add the garlic and all the wild mushrooms, apart from the black trumpets.

Season with a little salt and pepper, add the boiled wine, cover with a lid and cook at a full boil for a further minute.

Add the lemon juice and stir in the remaining butter. Lastly, add the black trumpets, the chopped parsley leaves and diced tomatoes; cook for a further 10 seconds, no more. Taste and correct the seasoning.

The essence of this dish is speed. If overcooked, the mushrooms release all their juice and lose all their texture. The dish becomes soupy. Add the black trumpets at the very last minute as they cook very quickly. Also, they would paint the dish black with their colour.

Serve in a large bowl or 4 soup plates, scatter the croutons over and finish with a little parsley.

Raymond Blanc OBE is chef patron of Le Manoir aux Quat'Saisons, a broadcaster and author of several books including Simply Raymond: Recipes from Home

SOUSED MACKEREL

I grew up at West Bay on the Dorset coast and, as a kid, I would sit on the harbour wall and watch the fishing boats and trawlers unload their catch onto the quay. I loved everything about the sea, with its mysterious and changing character, sometimes calm and unthreatening, sometimes so angry that it sent waves crashing over the promenade.

My dad had a house overlooking the bay and, in summer, I remember looking out to sea and watching the water boiling with shoals of mackerel. They were dead simple to catch. My friends and I would sit on the end of the pier with a super-light trout spinning rod and a tiny freshwater float. Holidaymakers would be casting huge beach casters over our heads, loaded with six or eight feather lures, but that wasn't our idea of fun. We wanted a bit more sport.

Even with our light single-hook tack, it didn't take long to catch enough fish to half fill a carrier bag. I would take them home to my gran, who would fry some of them up that night, split down the middle and floured. I loved watching them curl up in the pan, they were so fresh. We would eat them with a buttered chunk of homemade bread.

Whatever was left, my gran would souse in vinegar and leave in a bowl in the fridge to snack on for the rest of the week, the vinegar and pickled vegetables a delicious foil to the oily flesh.

I've always respected the humble mackerel for its eating qualities – as well as the sporty action it provides when fishing. I now have a boat at Lyme Regis, a few miles along the coast, and take my daughter out mackerel fishing in the bay to enjoy the same experience I had when I was young.

SERVES 4

2 mackerel, weighing about 250g, filleted, trimmed and boned

2 small shallots, peeled and cut into thin rings

1 small carrot, peeled and thinly sliced on the angle

1 bay leaf

10 black peppercorns

1 tsp sea salt

1 tsp fennel seeds

100ml cider vinegar

water to cover

Preheat the oven to 180C/160C Fan/Gas 4. Roll up the mackerel fillets skin-side out and secure each with a cocktail stick. Put them into an ovenproof dish, not too close together. Bring the rest of the ingredients to the boil in a saucepan and pour over the mackerel, then add enough water to just cover the fillets. Cover the dish with a lid or foil and cook in the oven for 2-3 minutes. Leave to cool in the dish. Serve with brown bread and butter.

Mark Hix MBE is a chef, restaurateur and food writer. He is the owner of The Oyster and Fish House in Lyme Regis and director of food and beverage at The Groucho Club

Rosie Sykes

BACON AND EGG PIE

My mum was a Kiwi and, when I was growing up, she had a dog-eared cookbook entitled *Edmonds Sure to Rise*. We baked a lot from it in my youth and I still have a version that I dip into regularly.

Mention it to any New Zealander and they will tell you which recipes are their favourites. Ours were Afghan biscuits (a chocolate cornflake biscuit with chocolate icing), hokey pokey biscuits (thrilling to make, as they involved adding bicarbonate of soda to hot milk, which would fizz and go volcanic), Loch Katrin cake (a pastry base covered with jam, currants, a layer of sponge and lemon icing) and, of course, bacon and egg pie.

Most Kiwi homes have a version of this New Zealand classic. The basic premise is two layers of puff-pastry sandwiched around cracked eggs and a layer of bacon, but there are many variations and additions. Peas are popular, as are tinned asparagus, sliced tomatoes, herbs... I have been known to add some blobs of herb-and-garlic cream cheese to make a vegetarian version.

Mum always made it on an enamel plate, which I still have and use. It came on picnics with us and she would wrap the pie in newspaper straight from the oven to keep it hot until lunchtime. I remember it as always being slightly soggy and tasting of the paper, which I know may not sound great, but it really, really was.

At my first solo cooking venture, a pub in Smithfield called The Sutton Arms, I put the pie on the menu as a bar snack, cooked as an individual portion in a little black steel frying pan. It was so popular we could hardly keep up with the pastry making. It now lives on at Towpath, a café-restaurant on the canal in East London where I often work. It's a dreamy spot with a wonderful community that has grown up around it. The tiny kitchen puts out plates and plates of breakfast and lunch and "The Pie" often graces the counter, alongside a wondrous selection of cakes, buns and biscuits, while the kitchen transitions between the two. Laura Jackson, Towpath's head chef, serves the pie with my rhubarb ketchup, which works very well indeed.

SERVES 4

200g puff pastry

a nut of butter, to grease the tin

5 eggs

5 rashers smoked back bacon, de-rinded (my mum always fried the rinds up to put on the bird table)

sea salt and black pepper

1 egg, beaten, to glaze

Preheat the oven to 220C/200C Fan/Gas 7. Preheat an oven tray, too: you want the pie to hit a nice hot tray so the bottom starts crisping immediately.

Roll out the puff pastry and cut into two – one half for the bottom, one for the top. Use the butter to grease a 24cm metal cake tin or preferably an enamel or Pyrex pie plate. Line the base with the pastry, draping it well over the edge and pressing well into the base.

Crack each egg into the pie dish – sometimes with the last one I hold back a bit of the egg white as it seems like too much white.

Get a small bladed sharp knife and prick each yolk to break it slightly, add a good dose of seasoning, then lay the rashers of bacon on top. Paint the rim of the pie with the egg white that you've held back or just dip your pastry brush in the pie. Before you put the lid on, paint it with the reserved egg white or by dipping a brush into the depths of the pie, then cut a cross in the middle of the lid and apply it to the pie. Press the edges together well. Trim off the excess overhanging pastry and crimp the edges. I'm a big fan of a big blousy crimp.

For the easiest crimp, run your thumb around the joined edges of the pie so that the joined edge isn't sticking to the pie dish. Now press the pastry with one finger outwards into the waiting pinch of finger and thumb of the other hand – this will create a scallop effect. Brush the top of the pastry with beaten egg.

Put the pie on the hot tray and turn the oven down to 200C/180C Fan/Gas 6 and leave the pie to cook for about 20 minutes, by which time the eggs will be set, the bacon cooked and the crust golden.

When you take the pie out of the oven, slide it out of the plate onto a wire rack so the crisp bottom you have engineered doesn't start steaming in the dish and go soggy (unless you are trying to recreate my childhood version, which is also marvellous). Serve it hot or warm. I tend to just serve it with chutney or ketchup, but buttered peas or a salad would work.

Rosie Sykes is a chef, food writer and author of The Sunday Night Book *and* Roasting Pan Suppers

Melissa Hemsley

FILIPINO-STYLE VEGETABLE SOUP

This gingery Filipino soup sums up my childhood. My dad was in the army, so we moved home – and school – a lot. But this soup was always a constant, something we ate once a week when we were growing up. It followed my mum from the Philippines, where she was born, to the UK, where she came to study in her twenties, then back and forth to Germany a few times, before finally settling in suburban south-west London.

It's classic Filipino comfort food. The traditional version uses one precious bird to flavour bowl after bowl of broth and many other meals besides. My mum said she'd always make sure she ate the chicken scraps, saving the "best bits" for her kids, so we could grow strong.

Though I love it best with chicken broth, this is a plant-based version. It's very versatile and the key is to pack it with onions, garlic and ginger and let everyone customise it themselves with the extra side sauce.

If you've got any leftover cooked chicken from a roast, you can add this in, too. It would also be lovely served with rice or noodles. My mum often served it with potatoes.

2 medium white/yellow onions, diced

1 ½ tbsp coconut oil or ghee

5 fat cloves of garlic, finely chopped

20g/1 fat thumb ginger, finely grated or chopped

150g/2 large carrots, halved and cut across into medium half moons

600g courgettes/potatoes/squash/sweet potato, sliced medium thick or chopped into 2cm pieces as appropriate

400g greens, such as pak choy or spinach

1 litre vegetable stock/organic chicken broth (if not veggie)

1½-2 tbsp tamari or soy sauce, to taste

2 tsp fish sauce (if not veggie) or extra tamari

juice of ¼ lemon

good pinch of pepper (white pepper if you have some)

cooked noodles or quinoa (optional)

For the extra pouring sauce

2 tbsp tamari or soy sauce

2 tbsp lemon juice

large pinch of (white) pepper

chopped fresh red chilli, optional

In a large saucepan, gently fry the onions, garlic and ginger in the oil for about 10 minutes until softened. Use the time to chop everything else.

Turn up the heat, add the carrots and squash/sweet potato (if using) and sea salt and pepper. Fry for a few minutes, then add the stock/broth, pop the lid on, bring to the boil and reduce to a medium simmer for 5 minutes.

Add the courgettes (if using) and cook for another 10 minutes until the veg are just tender.

Add the greens, tamari and fish sauce for a final few minutes (plus the cooked quinoa/noodles if using).

Season to taste with the pepper – you might not need salt because of the salty tamari and fish sauce – and serve up each bowl, letting everyone add their own extra sauce as they see fit.

Melissa Hemsley is a self-taught chef and writer who has written five cookbooks, including Feel Good

Henrietta Lovell

RUNNER BEANS WITH GARLIC AND TOMATO

One day, my father stood up from his deck chair, picked up a spade and started digging up the lawn. I thought he was looking for treasure. Or a body. In fact, he had decided that what our small South London garden really needed was a vegetable patch.

There wasn't much room behind the ancient, squeaking swings, but by the following summer, the tiny plot had filled with lettuces, radishes, courgettes, carrots, a deep cluster of potatoes and the runner beans my mother planted to hide the hole in the lawn. Their tendrils snaked up the swing frame, with thick green foliage and bright red flowers. You had to venture in deep to find the beans, which hung quietly in the shade of the leaves.

As children, we weren't allowed to open the fridge or the biscuit tin, not even the bread bin. Food was served at mealtimes and orange squash was all that was permitted in between. But when the runner beans ripened, they were ours to take as we pleased, straight from the vine, the sweetest, most delicious prize. The problem came when we missed one in its youth and it became old and tough and stringy – not good for eating raw. My mother boiled these ancient specimens just long enough to make them even tougher. I hated them.

But true love always finds a way. Many years later, at Superiority Burger in New York, I was given a dish of slow-cooked runner beans by the chef Brooks Headley. It was something I would never have ordered, but he just gave them to me to try. I am still learning not to trust my prejudices. It turns out that runner beans aren't only wonderful when they are young and fresh and crunchy. Stewed for hours, they become the tenderest, most toothsome delight in a new and extraordinary way.

SERVES 4

(as a main course with buttery mashed potatoes)

3 medium onions

8 cloves of garlic

2-3 sprigs of thyme

pinch chilli flakes

8-10 medium ripe tomatoes

2 tbsp tomato purée

12-14 runner beans, sliced into 5cm lengths

500ml water

salt and pepper

½ tin borlotti beans (you could use baked beans if that's all you have)

This dish is perfect just the way it is, but I have also made it with finely diced chorizo sausages, and it was delicious.

Slice the onions and add them to a heavy-based pot with a splash of oil. Cook until they soften a little, then add the whole cloves of garlic (with the chorizo, if you're using it) and allow them to turn golden.

Chop the tomatoes and add them in with everything else, except the borlotti beans, to putter along on a very low heat with the lid on for 2½-3 hours. Check now and then to see if it needs a splash more water.

After 1 ½ hours add the borlotti beans.

That's it. So easy. So very good. It also pairs wonderfully with an iced lemon verbena tea.

Henrietta Lovell is the founder and owner of the Rare Tea Company

Paul Ainsworth

GRANNY AINSWORTH'S CHIP BUTTY

Every Saturday night, from the age of about five, I'd go and stay over at my gran's. I have the best memories of just the two of us watching amazing, back-to-back programmes, like *Knight Rider*, *The A-Team* and *CHiPs* – and my gran always making me a chip butty. It was the simplicity of the freshly-baked white loaf, cut by hand, slathered with proper butter, hot salted chips and tomato ketchup. I loved the way the chips would melt the butter into the ketchup – it tasted so good. These days, I know it was the acidity from the ketchup that worked really well with the fat of the butter and the chips, but at five years old you don't think of that. Whenever I have a chip butty now, it reminds me of one of my absolute favourite and earliest food memories.

SERVES 1

2 slices sourdough

150g thick-cut steak chips

1 egg with a rich golden yolk

10g grated Parmesan

10g grated Cheddar

Salt and vinegar, to taste

For the rapeseed oil mayonnaise

100g egg yolk

35g Dijon mustard

35ml white wine vinegar

5g fine salt

40ml lemon juice

500ml rapeseed oil (to
    preferred consistency)

For the tomato fondue

5 banana shallots, finely diced

1 x 400g tin of tomatoes

vegetable oil

large handful of picked thyme

2 cloves grated garlic

80g light brown sugar

80ml sherry vinegar

Add all the mayo ingredients, except the oil, to a mixer. Turn it on and slowly add the oil to emulsify and thicken.

Soft boil your egg in boiling water for 6½ minutes and place straight into iced water. Let cool, then peel, slice in half and scoop your yolk out (this should be still runny but set enough to cut). Dice your yolk and fold through your mayonnaise, place this in a piping bag and then pipe back into your egg white.

For the tomato fondue, sweat the shallots in the vegetable oil with the garlic and picked thyme. Season with salt. When the shallots are soft and translucent, add the brown sugar and lightly caramelise. Then deglaze with the sherry vinegar. Add the tomatoes and cook slowly, uncovered, until reduced to a thick consistency. Taste and adjust with sherry vinegar and seasoning.

To assemble your chip butty, lightly toast the sourdough using a griddle pan, barbeque or chargrill. Then spread your tomato fondue on one side of each slice. Fry your chips in a deep fat fryer at 180C until golden and crispy. Place your chips on a cloth, making sure you remove as much oil from the chips as possible. Move to a mixing bowl and season with salt and vinegar, then toss with both grated cheeses. Layer the chips on your sourdough, place the top on your sandwich and finish off with the egg.

Paul Ainsworth is chef proprietor of Paul Ainsworth at Number 6 in Padstow, Cornwall

Hélène Darroze

DAUBE DE CÈPES

Ceps coming into season has always been a highlight of the year in households across the Landes region in south-western France. My family was no stranger to this enthusiasm and, every day that this valuable mushroom grew, my grandmothers were waiting. For Grandmother Charlotte, the highlight was my grandfather returning from the woods with the precious treasure; for Grandmother Louise, it was the dawn of the day when farmers would come back from the fields and sell their harvest in our restaurant kitchen.

They both loved the mushrooms, but nevertheless there was a connoisseur's disagreement between them over this iconic dish from Landaise gastronomy: *la daube de cèpes*. The base for this dish is shallots and ham, but mostly white wine, and that was the point of discord between them: Louise was adamant about the use of dry wine while Charlotte favoured a sweeter wine. This friendly quarrel had us in stitches many times over the years.

SERVES 6

1kg fresh ceps (penny bun
   mushrooms/porcini)

6 shallots

2 cloves of garlic, chopped

1 bouquet garni

200g jambon de pays or
   Bayonne ham

750ml dry white wine
   (or sweet white wine)

1 litre chicken stock

60g duck fat

salt

piment d'espelette

Wipe any dirt from the ceps using a damp cloth, then separate the heads from the stems. Finely slice the stems.

Dice the shallots and finely chop the ham, then stir together in a deep frying pan with half the duck fat until the shallots have softened. Add the chopped mushroom stems and garlic.

Leave to cook down for 10 minutes or so, then tip in the white wine and simmer gently on a low heat for about 20 minutes until the wine has almost evaporated.

Meanwhile, cut the heads of the ceps into 1cm slices. Heat the remaining duck fat in a frying pan, add the sliced ceps and season with salt and piment d'espelette. Cook until the mushrooms are well browned.

Pour the chicken stock onto the chopped stalk mixture, add the cep slices and bouquet garni, then simmer gently for about 1 hour.

When the daube is ready, adjust the seasoning with salt and a pinch of piment d'espelette.

Hélène Darroze has six Michelin stars across her three restaurants in London, Paris and Provence, winning three for Hélène Darroze at The Connaught in 2021

Caroline Gilmartin

PISSALADIÈRE

The 1970s was a curious time for food. Growing up in suburban London, I remember the excitement of two-foot-long spaghetti, soused not in rich anchovy butter or fresh basil pesto as it might be now, but in mince from a tin and unmistakably scented dried Parmesan. Findus crispy pancakes and Fray Bentos pies were also regular staples at the family dinner table. Convenience foods seemed very exciting at the time – little did we know what they would later do to the health of the nation.

But every now and then Mum would dig out her Cordon Bleu Cookery Course and excel herself. The series came in 72 weekly parts and I'd spend hours poring over the booklets, imagining all the feasts that could be had. Many of the covers are etched upon my memory: the wire egg basket one, the "cooking for the church fête" one, and No 70, with its curious subheadings: Invalid Trays and Health Foods. Mum assures me that she will bequeath them to me in her will.

From within those pages came this recipe for pissaladière. This dish is often made on a bread-dough base, similar to pizza, but here it has been recreated as a flan and is none the worse for it. Mum's scribbles denote various changes she has made to the recipe, which in turn I've tweaked over the years. Now it's your turn – further embellish as you wish.

For the pastry

85g wholemeal flour

75g white flour

50g Parmesan, grated

75g cold cubed butter

2-3 tbsp iced water to mix

For the filling

400g fresh tomatoes (for oven roasting – substitute with tinned if you need to)

salt and pepper

olive oil

3 garlic cloves, crushed

1kg red onions, sliced very finely in rounds

English mustard

tomato purée

Parmesan

tinned anchovies in oil

pitted olives (green or black), sliced

Slice the tomatoes in half, season with salt, pepper and a third of the garlic, then douse in olive oil and oven roast at 180C/160C Fan/Gas 4 for about an hour.

While the tomatoes are cooking, mix the pastry ingredients in a food processor until breadcrumby, then pulse in iced water 1 tbsp at a time until the crumbs can be pressed together between thumb and forefinger.

Tip the pastry into a 25cm flan case and press down onto the base with your fingers or a small rolling pin. Put in the fridge or freezer while you cook the onions.

Put a good slug of olive oil into a frying pan and add the onions and the garlic. Cook very slowly over a low heat until they are completely soft, stirring now and then. This might take 40 minutes.

Take the tomatoes from the oven (leave the oven on) and add them (or the tinned tomatoes) to the onions, removing the skins if they bother you. Cook for another 15 minutes or so until the juice has been reduced and the mix is fairly dry. Season with salt and pepper to taste.

Get the pastry case out of the fridge and smear the base with about 1 tablespoon of English mustard. Next, add the same amount of tomato purée and a sprinkling of Parmesan.

Press the onion mixture firmly into the flan case and level the surface with a spoon. Arrange the anchovies in a criss-cross pattern on top and put a slice of olive in every square.

Cook for about half an hour, in the middle of the oven, until the pastry is cooked, but before the top gets burnt. Serve warm.

Bristol-based Dr Caroline Gilmartin is a fermenter, writer and a member of the Wild & Well festival collective

Marcus Fergusson

CREMA DE FRIJOL

I've been obsessed with cheese for as long as I can remember. I was such a precocious and gluttonous child that I requested cheese fondue for my sixth birthday party. I tucked in with gusto, lifting prongfuls of crusty bread and liquefied Gruyère to my mouth until I was fit to burst. Then I ate some more until, quite suddenly, I felt unwell. I just managed to make it to the bathroom before I was copiously sick.

My mother cleaned me up and dressed me in my pyjamas. I put on a dressing gown and returned downstairs to the fondue pot to scrape up the last morsels of what, by now, was quite solid cheese until there was nothing left.

As I grew older, my cheese adventures continued. I devoured macaroni cheese made with orange Scottish Cheddar and would watch with delight as cheese on toast slowly bubbled and blistered under the grill. I experienced the joy of a proper brie de meaux that had been allowed to sit on a Provençal windowsill and the pleasure of cutting into a hunk of Emmenthal and discovering the hidden holes. As a teenager, I moved onto the hard stuff – literally in the case of Parmesan – but also Roquefort, Gorgonzola, Stilton and Époisses de Bourgogne. As I hit my twenties, I sought out cheeses on holiday that couldn't, at the time, be found in Britain: Banon and Saint-Marcellin in France, even gjetost in Norway.

On one occasion, I met up with two cheese-loving work colleagues at the Harrods Cheese Bar. We were told that, despite their impressive range, only three cheeses were available to taste. Shocked, one colleague called over the manager, pointed at me and said, "Do you know who this is? This is the President of the London Cheese Club." The manager was impressed: "I've been wanting to meet someone like you. I'm new in the job and I want to make some changes. Perhaps organise some events. How many members do you have?" I stonewalled: "I'm afraid that's classified. But I'm sure we could do something. We should talk further."

The manager gave us free rein to taste whatever cheese we wanted, and we sat happily at the bar for an hour after the shop had closed, before he walked us to the door and let us out. The London Cheese Club was born.

Many years later, I decided to harness my obsession and started making cheeses of my own. One of them is a queso fresco, a Mexican-inspired soft cheese, which is perfect for the recipe here.

2 x 400g tins of black beans (or 200g dried beans, soaked overnight)

2 medium tomatoes, roughly chopped

1 onion, roughly chopped

4 garlic cloves, roughly chopped

½ tsp cumin

1 tsp salt

½ tsp cloves

To garnish

1 avocado, cubed

sour cream

100g queso fresco, cubed

2 tbsp chopped coriander

3 corn tortillas

1 large ancho chilli

1 lime, juiced

Rinse the beans and put them in a large saucepan with the tomatoes, onion, garlic, cumin, salt and cloves. Add enough water to cover the ingredients by about 4cm.

Boil and simmer for 40-50 minutes, until the beans are tender. Make sure the water does not boil dry.

Meanwhile, cut the tortillas into strips, 2.5cm thick and about 7cm long. Fry gently in vegetable oil until crisp, then dry on kitchen paper. Repeat with the ancho chilli.

Remove the cloves then whizz the soup in a food processor until very smooth and return to the saucepan to reheat.

Stir in the lime and ladle into bowls. Add a swirl of sour cream and a sprinkling of each of the garnishes, except for the tortillas, which should be served on the side. If you like, you can add a swirl of your favourite hot sauce, too.

Marcus Fergusson makes award-winning new-wave cheeses in Somerset, including Renegade Monk, Rebel Nun, Gert Lush and a queso fresco, La Fresca Margarita

Ed Smith

CHEESY LEEKS

My childhood wasn't quite a "shelling peas on nonna's knee" cliché. I got into cooking because I realised that if I helped Mum make Sunday lunch, it would be my brothers (and Dad) on washing-up duty. Other regular visitors to our table were: spag bol; chilli con carne (same as spag bol, plus kidney beans and not much chilli powder); and cottage pie (spag bol, plus mashed potato.) It must be the same for many children of 1980s Britain.

However, I also fondly remember "cheesy leeks": blanched leeks buried beneath a béchamel blanket. I can picture a large, rectangular Pyrex dish of them sitting in the middle of the plastic tablecloth, with a tray of baked potatoes providing enough ballast to shut up four hungry boys.

This is basically that dish... although I'm fairly sure Mum didn't use Alpine cheese. It's excellent alongside pork and lamb, roast chicken, beef, squash and aubergine, too. Enjoy with a sharply dressed bitter-leaf salad and boiled new potatoes.

SERVES 4

- 3 trimmed leeks (about 400g)
- 25g butter
- 25g plain flour
- 300ml whole milk
- ½ tsp Dijon mustard
- ¼ tsp flaky sea salt
- ¼ tsp ground black pepper
- 60g Alpine cheese (Comté, Gruyère), grated
- 60g breadcrumbs from sourdough or similar
- 1 tbsp cold-pressed rapeseed oil

Bring a pan of salted water to a boil. Cut the leeks into 3cm thick rounds and plunge into cold water, to wash away any mud. Transfer to the pan and gently simmer until just tender (6-8 minutes), then drain.

Meanwhile, in a small pan, melt the butter over a low-medium heat, add the flour and stir in. Continue to stir until the paste slackens (but doesn't colour), then whisk in the milk 2-3 tablespoons at a time, ensuring it's absorbed before adding the next load.

Cook the white sauce for 5 minutes, stirring occasionally, to thicken. Add the mustard, salt, pepper and two thirds of the cheese. Stir until melted, then remove from the heat.

Arrange the leeks in any ovenproof baking dish in which they fit snugly in one layer – probably with ¾–1 litre capacity. Pour the cheese sauce over them. Mix the breadcrumbs with the oil, then scatter them over the cheesy leeks. Finish with the rest of the grated cheese.

When ready to eat, bake for around 20 minutes in an oven preheated to 220C/200C Fan/Gas 8, until bubbling and golden brown.

Ed Smith is an award-winning cook and food writer. He is the author of three cookbooks – On the Side, The Borough Market Cookbook *and* Crave *– and the food blog rocketandsquash.com*

Gill Meller

MINESTRONE SOUP

People often ask how I got into cooking. Depending on the exact question, my answer begins in one of two ways. If I'm asked "Why did you start cooking?" I'll say "Because I was 18 and really needed the money." But if the question is "What made you want to be a chef?" I'll answer "Because my mum taught me to love good food."

My mum loved cooking – I mean really loved it – and she was excellent at it, too. It wasn't that her food was elaborate or technical. She would make simple, homely dishes – roast chicken, kedgeree, seasonal soups, shepherd's pie, spag bol, sausages, mash and onion gravy, grilled fish and sauté potatoes, liver and bacon, fish pie – all prepared with the same love and care.

She not only cared about where her ingredients had come from, she cared about seasonality (this was the 1980s, when few people talked about such things).

But beyond this, she cared about taste. For her, the taste of a dish was everything, the basis for all joy found in eating. I recall her concentrating as she cooked, thinking about how things might be improved. I remember the constant tasting, from the spoon, and the subtle changes in her expression in response to the particular level of deliciousness she was experiencing.

Interestingly, I didn't actually learn to cook from my mum, at least not in the way a student is taught by their teacher. But everything she did I seemed to take in subconsciously. Through her, I learned to value ingredients and to savour taste, and that the simplest approach is nearly always the best.

She taught me to use my senses and how to feel my way through a recipe until it looked, smelt and tasted the way I wanted. Her approach gave me a freedom in the kitchen and the confidence to follow my instincts. It's very rare that I cook from a recipe today. So many of the things mum made I have learned to cook from my memory. Soups, like this minestrone – which she made regularly and I absolutely loved – left such an impression on me that words, weights and measures were unnecessary. Instead, I can close my eyes and see her making it. I see the different vegetables and herbs, her dark oval chopping board and the heavy pan warming on the stove. I see how it is built up, in layers. I see the size of the little bubbles that rise to the surface as the soup simmers gently away. I remember the beans, the olive oil and the colour. And, most importantly, I remember the taste, texture and balance she was able to achieve between the ingredients.

3 tbsp extra virgin olive oil, plus
   extra to serve

1 large onion, chopped

3 or 4 carrots, peeled and cut
   into 4-5mm (¼in) cubes

4 tender sticks celery, sliced

4 garlic cloves, thinly sliced

3 or 4 bay leaves

2 x 400g tins good-quality plum
   tomatoes

2 litres vegetable stock

1 x 400g tin of haricot beans,
   drained and rinsed

100g spaghetti

1 bunch of kale, chard or
   spinach, tougher stalks
   removed and leaves roughly
   chopped

¼ savoy cabbage, thinly
   shredded

1 small bunch of parsley, leaves
   picked and chopped

grated Parmesan, to serve

salt and freshly ground black
   pepper

Heat a large heavy-based pan over a medium heat and add the olive oil. When it's hot, add the onion, carrots, celery, garlic and bay. Season with salt and pepper. Cook gently, stirring regularly, until the vegetables begin to soften and smell sweet, about 10 minutes. Adjust the heat if you need to so that the vegetables don't colour.

Empty the tinned tomatoes into a bowl and use your hands to crush them thoroughly, then tip them into the pan with the soft vegetables. Cook, stirring occasionally, for 15-20 minutes, then add the vegetable stock and bring to a simmer. Allow the soup to cook gently for about 45 minutes, then add the haricot beans. Break the spaghetti into short lengths and add that, too. Return the pan to a simmer and cook for a further 30 minutes, then add the kale, chard or spinach and cabbage and stir well.

Give the soup a final 15-20 minutes' cooking, until all the vegetables are tender. If at any point it is looking too thick, add some water. Taste the soup and adjust the seasoning with salt and pepper, then stir in the parsley.

I like to take the pan off the heat and let the soup stand at this point: I think it benefits from 15-20 minutes just being, before you ladle it into bowls and serve trickled with plenty of your best olive oil and scattered with finely grated Parmesan cheese.

Don't worry if you don't eat it all in one sitting. This minestrone (and others like it) can taste even better the following day.

Gill Meller is a chef, food writer and author of cookbooks including Outside: Recipes for a Wilder Way of Eating

Ruth Rogers

CORN POLENTA

Growing up in a farming community in upstate New York meant that we ate by the seasons and, of all the produce that grows there, it is the corn that I remember the most. We'd buy it fresh, picked right before taking it home to eat. If we had corn for lunch, we'd go buy it in the morning. If the corn was for supper, we'd buy it in the afternoon. Once home, we'd sit down to husk the corn and then it was boiled, for 5 minutes or so, until it was just done. We ate simply at home and that went for the corn too. We'd eat it just as it came, slathered in lots of melting butter, with sea salt sprinkled on top. That's what I think about when I think of eating corn.

Other than the excitement of eating the corn, going to collect it meant that we would go to town. On the way we would pass by the post office or else there'd be other errands to run and this meant social interaction. Back then, Woodstock was a small, quiet town. We didn't have bars, restaurants or cafés and so we'd fight to be the one to go pick up the post, because it was a chance to talk with people, people we knew, people who lived and worked there.

We'd chat with the farmer too, who'd always peel back the husks so that we could see that the kernels inside were small, young and juicy, just as they should be. To this day, I only ever eat corn like that, from farms back in upstate New York. Those varieties are so fine and sweet, there's nowhere else that grows it quite like that.

We cried when the corn season was over. It meant the trips were over, too.

Happily, I've found that the people of northern Italy have an equal respect and love for the many varieties of seasonal corns that go into making polenta. In polenta season, we make it every day here at The River Café and I love it!

SERVES 6-8

350g coarse polenta

1 tsp sea salt

150g unsalted butter, softened

200g Parmesan, grated

Put the polenta in a jug so that it can be poured in a steady stream.

Bring 1.75 litres water to the boil in a large saucepan and add the salt. Lower the heat to a simmer and slowly add the polenta, stirring with a whisk until completely blended. It will now start to bubble volcanically.

Reduce the heat to as low as possible, cover with a lid and cook the polenta for 40-45 minutes, stirring from time to time with a wooden spoon to prevent a skin from forming. The polenta is cooked when it falls away from the sides of the pan and has become very dense and thick.

Stir in the butter and Parmesan and season generously with sea salt and black pepper.

Ruth Rogers CBE is a chef and writer who co-founded The River Café in London. Her books include The River Café Cookbook *and* River Café Simple Italian

Jeremy Lee

LENTIL SOUP

When I was growing up, I didn't have school lunches. Instead, I'd go to my grandmother's house in Dundee every day. Her name was Jessie Dorothy Stewart and she was a very canny Scotswoman, with a small but good repertoire of dishes we all loved: amazing mince and tatties, with beautiful, cloud-like suet dumplings (which I've never been able to replicate), a wonderful treacle dumpling – a suet pudding we were all mad for – and her lentil soup, which we were similarly passionate about.

My grandmother was tragically widowed when I was very young – she was only in her late 50s or early 60s. I was one of four children, so she played a huge part in raising us. Having lots of grandchildren to look after was very important to her. It gave her a sense of purpose.

My grandmother's lentil soup is a very dour Scottish dish: plain, good, ordinary, fine cooking. Just the thing to warm the soul and heart and belly. It's something for cold days – not to have at the height of summer. That said, when the sun goes down in Scotland, even in the summer, a hot broth is just what you want.

This was the first dish that made me aware that cooking is about hearth and home. As it simmered for hours on the hob, it filled the house with a wonderful embracing warmth. It's a lingering memory that I treasure. We'd have it with lots of crusty bread, fresh from Fisher & Donaldson's bakery down the road (which is still going strong) and lots of butter. Shocking amounts of butter really – we were all the size of houses. There was a grocer on the Perth Road in Dundee and you could get him to carve off a slice of butter, knock it into a pat and wrap it in paper to bring home.

I know the recipe for her soup off by heart. It's actually more a collection of ingredients thrown in a pan. I still make it on the rare occasions I manage to get out of the restaurant. I'll go to the butcher's for the smoked ham hock, and a good Indian deli for orange lentils that haven't been sitting on the shelf for years. You need a tiny little nut of lard to start the proceedings off, then you add the veg, the ham and enough water to come two-thirds of the way up the pan, and leave it to tick over for three, four hours, sometimes five. Sometimes my grandmother would make it the night before, then leave it to settle, and the lentils would break down. She made everything seem effortless.

SERVES 6-8

1 nugget of lard

6-8 carrots, roughly chopped

2 potatoes, roughly chopped

1-2 celery stalks, roughly
chopped

1-2 leeks, roughly chopped

2 onions, roughly chopped

200g red split lentils, rinsed

1 ham hock

2 bay leaves

a few sprigs of fresh parsley

salt and black pepper

Fry the vegetables in the lard in a large, deep pan for 10 minutes or so, until softened. Add the lentils and fry for a couple of minutes, stirring, then add the ham hock and enough water to cover plus a bit more. Add the herbs, bring to the boil, then turn down the heat.

Skim any froth from the surface and simmer, covered, but with the lid slightly askew to let out excess steam, for a minimum of 2 hours and as long as 4 or 5. Top up with water as necessary until the ham is cooked through. Don't put in too much water, as this is a thick soup: you can always add more at the end to thin it out.

Take out the hock and herbs and set aside. Take out a third to a half of the soup, blend it, then pour that back into the pan. Return it to the hob to heat through, stirring to combine.

Shred the ham and put it back into the soup, or serve separately. Finish with lots of chopped parsley, a little salt if necessary (the hock will give the soup quite a lot), and plenty of black pepper.

Jeremy Lee was head chef at Blueprint Café for many years and is now chef patron of Quo Vadis in London. He recently published his first cookbook, Cooking Simply and Well, For One or Many

Jane Baxter

CICERI E TRIA

This dish, from Puglia in the south of Italy, represents everything I love about real Italian food. No blobs or dubious scrapings, just a bowl of pure, undiluted, unpretentious joy. It wasn't part of my own childhood, but it symbolises some of the happiest times I have spent with my son David as he has grown up.

I have been lucky enough to visit Puglia many times, meeting some remarkable people, chefs and producers and experiencing their great hospitality. Since he was young, David has come with me. These trips have always been a special time for us, a chance to sit and share meals, a rare occurrence at home, and simply to enjoy each other's company.

The city of Lecce, known as the Florence of the south, is particularly dear to us both. It was there that David developed his worrying addiction to *pasticciotto*, the local custard pies made with lard pastry; and where he learnt to love vongole, mussels and squid and all the pasta dishes you associate with southern Italy. When he was little, restaurants would set up a makeshift bed for him next to the table, so he could sleep contentedly as the grown-ups sat eating, drinking and talking long into the night.

Hidden in the back streets of the city is a place we return to again and again: a restaurant called Alle Due Corti. The menu is written entirely in local dialect and features simple Pugliese fare, cooked by the owner Rosalba and served by members of her family. David still ranks Rosalba's meatballs as one of his favourite dishes of all time. But it is this chickpea pasta ("*ciceri e tria*") for which the restaurant is particularly known. It brings together a few simple ingredients – pasta, chickpeas and olive oil – to create a dish that is a testament to the great food and cooks of Puglia.

It is a dish I have made and eaten too many times to count, and every time, I am transported back to this wonderful land and all the memories David and I have made there: eating the best pizza – made by our friend Maurizio – on the church steps in Lecce, sitting with an iced almond coffee outside Avio bar, David jumping into the sea at the Grotta della Poesia, watching the Passeggiata together in Trani. David is grown up now, but this place, and this dish, are things I will always associate with his childhood.

SERVES 4

250g dried chickpeas,
soaked overnight in plenty
of cold water

6 cloves garlic

½ leek

½ stick celery

½ red onion, peeled

2 cherry tomatoes

1 dried red chilli

1 sprig rosemary

150ml olive oil

1 sprig rosemary

4 cloves garlic

1 red chilli

extra virgin olive oil

2 tbsp chopped parsley

salt and pepper

For the pasta

200g fine semolina flour, plus
extra for rolling

100g pasta flour

pinch salt

150ml water

Drain the chickpeas and place in a pan. Cover with water and add the next 7 ingredients. Bring up to the boil and simmer for about an hour or until the chickpeas are tender. Keep the pulses covered with water during the cooking process. Season well when cooked.

While the chickpeas are cooking, make the pasta in a food processor. Tip in the fine semolina and pasta flour. Blitz with a little salt and slowly add the water until you have a soft, pliable dough. Knead for a few minutes, divide into 4 balls and pass each piece through a pasta machine up to setting number 6. This pasta is thicker than traditional egg pasta. Cut each strip into 8-10cm lengths about 1-2cm wide. Toss in semolina flour and leave on a tray until needed.

Remove the whole vegetables from the pan of chickpeas, discarding the rosemary. Put the vegetables in a food processor or liquidiser with 100ml of the cooking liquid and blitz to a smooth paste. Return to the pan and stir into the chickpeas.

Heat the oil in a pan with the garlic, rosemary and chilli until the garlic starts to brown. Remove from the pan with a slotted spoon (with the chilli and herbs) and tip in a third of the pasta strips. Stir-fry the pasta until crisp and lightly browned. Scoop onto kitchen roll with a slotted spoon. Tip chickpeas into oil and stir well.

Cook the rest of the pasta in salted boiling water for a few minutes. Drain well and stir through the soupy chickpeas. Season well and fold through parsley and good olive oil, along with half of the crunchy pasta. Transfer to a serving dish and top with the rest of the fried pasta.

Jane Baxter is a chef and food writer. A regular contributor to The Guardian *and author of several cookbooks, in 2005 she set up the Riverford Field Kitchen and now runs food and event company Wild Artichokes in Devon*

Rachel Khoo

WONTONS IN A SMOKY BACON BROTH

On my first trip to visit relatives in Malaysia, I remember an old Chinese man with a bike that had been turned into a mobile kitchen. He would ring his bell, a bit like an ice cream van, to let everyone know "The wonton man is here". People would come outside with empty bowls and return home with them full of steaming soup and savoury dumplings. This was the first time I had ever had noodle soup for breakfast – very different from the cereal or toast and jam I was used to growing up in the UK.

The older I get, the more I crave savoury soups, pickles and fermented foods for breakfast. Despite having lived for eight years in Paris, where the scent of freshly baked croissants wafts onto every neighbourhood *rue*, I would rather eat a bowl of steaming wonton soup any day.

Wonton soup is a classic Cantonese dish that found its way to Malaysia with the Chinese from Hong Kong and other parts of South China. It's traditionally made with chicken or vegetable stock, but my version uses a smoky bacon broth. The dumplings can be frozen for up to two months in an airtight container. Simply boil them for an additional 5 minutes.

SERVES 3-4

20-25 wonton skins (from Asian
supermarkets or online)

For the filling

125g raw prawns, shelled and
deveined

4 tbsp finely chopped bamboo
shoots

1 tsp spring onion (white
part only; save the rest for the
soup), finely chopped

1 tsp corn flour

½ tsp fine salt

½ tsp sugar

½ tsp sesame oil

½ tsp dry sherry

pinch of white pepper

For the broth

200g smoky bacon

1 litre cold water

1 tsp fine salt

pinch of sugar

For the garnish

2-4 tsp light soy sauce

1 spring onion, finely sliced

pickled or fresh chillies
(optional), thinly sliced

Mince the prawns and mix with the rest of the filling ingredients. This can be done up to a day in advance and kept in an airtight container in the fridge. Moisten the edges of a wonton skin with a little water and place a teaspoonful of filling into the centre. Twist to seal the edges. The wonton should resemble a money bag. Repeat until all the filling is used.

Put the smoky bacon, salt, sugar and cold water in a saucepan. Bring to a simmer and cook for 30 minutes. Pour through a fine sieve to remove the bacon.

Bring the strained broth to a simmer again and add the wontons. Cook for 5 minutes. Divide the soup and dumplings between the bowls. Garnish with finely sliced spring onions and a drizzle of soy sauce. For a spicy kick, serve with some chilli sauce.

If you're having this as a light lunch, add some roughly sliced pak choi or other green leafy vegetables at the same time as cooking the wontons.

Rachel Khoo is a cook, broadcaster and author of five cookbooks including The Little Paris Kitchen

Pooch Horsburgh

PRAWN COCKTAIL

My childhood summers were spent in the west of Ireland, where we'd decamp for a month or two. There were lots of children with very little supervision and we ran riot, spending our days climbing trees, swimming in Loch Corrib, making dens and camping out armed with an axe, a box of matches and a pack of sausages. I'm not sure today's parents would be so relaxed, but we lived to tell the tale and with only a few scars to show for it.

Mealtimes were filled with my mother's delicious renditions of our childhood favourites. I'm sure the grown-ups ate well, too – and doubtless drank excellent wine – but we were too busy upstairs plotting midnight feasts to notice.

As a treat, we'd collect fresh lobster from the local fishermen and watch them "sleeping" under a blanket of damp newspaper in the fridge. They were boiled in huge pots and we would listen in terror as they cooked, convinced that the lobsters were tapping on the lids to get out.

To mark the beginning of the holiday, we'd meet up with other families at Moran's Oyster Cottage, a thatched house beside a tidal river outside Galway, which was en route to the place we stayed. It is now rather smart and well known, but back then it felt like our secret.

On one Moran's outing, my Uncle Will played a trick on us. He hid an oyster in his napkin, pretended to do a huge sneeze into it, then paraded the contents around the table to screams of laughter mixed with horror from the children.

For the grown-ups, Moran's was all about the oysters. But for me, it was the prawn cocktail that I looked forward to most. My (Irish) mother would wax lyrical about freshly boiled Dublin Bay prawns and I think it must have been made with these; Irish prawn cocktails always tasted so much better than anything we had back home. It wasn't just the prawns themselves, but the bread and the butter served alongside. I'd eat the prawns and shredded iceberg lettuce first, then wipe up the remaining sauce with slices of bread spread with an extreme quantity of butter. The grown-ups would always be distracted, and nobody noticed quite how many pats of salted deliciousness I was getting through.

Prawn cocktail is still one of my favourite dishes, more often than not enjoyed with a spicy Bloody Mary on the side these days. Add some fries and you've got pretty much my ideal lunch. But those simple Irish prawn cocktails will always be close to my heart. This is my attempt at recreating them.

SERVES 2

300g cooked, whole, shell-on
    prawns

½ an iceberg lettuce, outer
    leaves removed

For the sauce

5 tbsp mayonnaise

1 tbsp tomato ketchup

¼ tsp brandy

a couple of shakes of
    Worcestershire sauce

pinch of cayenne pepper, plus a
    little extra for dusting

Tabasco, to taste

squeeze or two of lemon juice

sea salt and freshly ground black
    pepper

To serve

2 wedges of lemon

brown bread, sliced and cut into
    triangles

lots of Irish salted butter

Peel the prawns and leave to one side. If you want to look swish you could leave two unpeeled for garnish (although this definitely wasn't how they were served in Ireland during the late 1980s and early 1990s).

Shred the lettuce, favouring the whiter, crisper parts. If it is remotely limp then place in iced water to crisp up. Drain and dry really well with kitchen paper or a clean tea towel before using.

Mix together the sauce ingredients. Start with a small squeeze of lemon juice and a shake or two of Tabasco. Taste, then go from there, adding a little more of each or either to taste. Season with a little salt and pepper; it won't need much of either, but benefits from a touch of both.

Place a dollop of the sauce into the bottom of two martini glasses or serving dishes. Top with shredded lettuce, pushing it down into the glass/dish. Add the prawns on top, dividing them equally between the two glasses/dishes. Spoon the rest of the sauce over the prawns and dust the top with a little extra cayenne pepper. Attach a lemon wedge to the side of each glass/dish.

Serve with triangles of brown bread with lots of butter on the side. Alternatively, add fries and a spicy Bloody Mary for a brilliant lunch.

Pooch Horsburgh is a food stylist and cookbook author. Her latest book is The Forge Kitchen, *with Alex Pole*

Tom Kerridge

FISH-FINGER BUTTIES

This is a massive throwback to my childhood memories. As a chef, I find myself looking back at all the little touch points from the time when I first started cooking. I grew up in a single-parent family, and my mum had two jobs, so I used to cook tea for myself and my brother. Simple things like jacket potatoes and baked beans, with those little sausages. When you're 14, being able to cook something without setting fire to the kitchen gives you quite a sense of achievement. And my brother seemed to like what I cooked. A fish-finger sandwich was easy to do and was the start of my culinary adventures. Super tasty, it stands the test of time and it's something I look upon with warm nostalgia. Whether it is pre-sliced bread that sticks to the roof of your mouth or posh sourdough, fish-finger sandwiches are always a winner.

For the butties

12 fish fingers

8 slices of bread

spread

2 large tomatoes

4 potato waffles, optional

For the sweet cucumber ribbons

½ cucumber

1 tbsp malt vinegar

a pinch of sugar

For the coleslaw

¼ iceberg lettuce

1 carrot

2 tbsp mayonnaise

Whack the grill on high or put the oven on at 200C/180C Fan/Gas 6.

Start with the cucumber ribbons. Use a vegetable peeler to peel long, wide strips along the length of the cucumber. Pop into a bowl and drizzle with the vinegar and a pinch of sugar. Mix to combine and set aside.

Place the fish fingers (and waffles, if using) on a baking tray and cook for 20 minutes, turning halfway through.

Next, make the coleslaw. Thinly cut the lettuce and peel and grate the carrot, then put it all into a bowl. Add the mayonnaise and mix together to combine.

When the fish fingers are cooked, add the spread to the bread slices. Slice the tomato and lay onto 4 slices of the bread. Dollop a spoonful of coleslaw on top, then place 3 fish fingers on each, followed by a waffle, if using. Next, take a spoonful of the cucumber ribbons and drain off the liquid before topping each sandwich. Finally, place the remaining 4 slices of buttered bread onto each sandwich and gently squash them down. Cut the sandwiches in half and tuck in.

Tom Kerridge is a chef, restaurateur and broadcaster, whose restaurants include The Hand and Flowers in Marlow. His books include Outdoor Cooking *and* The Dopamine Diet

A version of this recipe appeared in Tom Kerridge and Marcus Rashford's 'Full Time', a campaign aimed at calling full time on child food poverty #EndChildFoodPoverty

Margot Henderson

SNAILS, SOBRASADA, OAKLEAF AND CROUTONS

My dad was very keen on smelly cheese and kept a pot of shucked oysters in the fridge to snack on. I had a feeling these things were quite exotic – something to be tried and enjoyed. When he had been gathering field mushrooms, I remember the smell of them frying in butter. I knew that if something smelt that good, then it must be good to eat. I was quite a greedy kid.

My introduction to French gastronomy came when I was nine years old, at Belmont Primary School in New Zealand. We were learning about France and our teacher announced that, as our next lesson, we were going to cook a classic French dish, *les escargots* – quite an unusual undertaking for kids in the suburbs of Wellington.

We were told to go out and collect a jar of snails from our garden – not a problem – then we drowned them and took them out of their shells. The next day our teacher fried them up with garlic, parsley and breadcrumbs. It smelt fantastic.

I was a daring child and I had no problem trying these morsels. Maybe it was the combination of fried garlic, parsley and butter – always a winner – but I loved them. I must have told my mum because, for my next birthday, I was given snails in tins with their shells, and I would cook them up for my mother's dinner parties. It became my thing: "Will Margot cook her snails?"

I still love a snail and often have them on the menu. One of our favourite snail dishes, which goes back to the days when we cooked at the French House in the 1990s, is a snail and oakleaf salad. The simple recipe is much loved and was given to us by Emily Green, a wonderful writer. The snails are cooked in garlic, shallots, a little chilli, white wine, parsley and thyme, then tossed in a salad of oak leaves and croutons with a mustard vinaigrette.

I don't gather snails from the garden any more. Instead, we buy British farmed snails from "the snail man". They arrive in bags of a hundred and we pop them in the freezer until they are needed. They are very happy frozen.

For the mustard dressing

1 tbsp Dijon or seeded mustard

1 tbsp red wine vinegar

Juice of ½ lemon

70ml extra virgin olive oil

For the salad

a few splashes olive oil

2 shallots, peeled and sliced into
thin half moons

4 cloves of garlic, peeled and
sliced or grated

a handful finely chopped thyme

100g sobrasada (optional), or
chorizo or trotter gear

1 dozen snails, cooked, without
shells

splash of red wine vinegar

splash of white wine

splash of chicken stock

a handful of picked and finely
chopped curly parsley

1 oakleaf lettuce, picked, washed
and spun

1 pinch of Maldon salt

black pepper

sourdough bread

Whisk together the vinegar, lemon and mustard, then slowly whisk in olive oil.

In a pan with a happy splash of olive oil, cook the shallots, garlic and thyme, then add the sobrasada. On a gentle heat, let them all get to know each other, stirring occasionally.

Add the wine, vinegar and stock and leave to simmer for a few moments – it should be wettish. Add the snails, season and cook for 8 minutes over a medium heat. Leave to the side.

Heat the oven to 180C/160C Fan/Gas 4.

Take rough hunks of sourdough and rip into uneven bits, then toss in olive oil and bake until nice and crisp.

To make the salad bring all your components together, toss and season.

Serve with a glass or two of Brouilly. A perfect lunch.

Margot Henderson OBE is a chef, caterer and food writer and co-owner of Arnold & Henderson and Rochelle Canteen in Shoreditch, and runs The Three Horseshoes in Somerset

Big Suppers

Gennaro Contaldo

SQUID IN TOMATO SAUCE

Although my father was the official cook in our house, there were certain dishes my mother cooked. One was squid. She always worried when I went fishing, but if I told her I was going to the rocks to catch calamari, she would get very excited and tell me to bring home lots. So off I would go, armed with my homemade harpoon and fishing line.

When I returned with a bucket full of squid, my mother's eyes would light up. She'd take the bucket from me and go into the kitchen to cook her special squid dish. She would cook immediately so as not to lose the fresh flavour of the sea. I would join my mother in the kitchen and sit and watch her cook, wondering if I would cook like her when I grew up.

I still make this dish today, in exactly the same way she did and when I do, it is as if she is watching over me and whispering "Be careful, not too much salt – there is enough salt in the sea!" This is delicious served with pasta such as linguine or spaghetti or simply with lots of good, rustic, toasted bread, topped with the squid and a drizzle of extra virgin olive oil. *Fantastico!*

SERVES 4-6

6 tbsp extra virgin olive oil

6 anchovy fillets

10g capers

2 garlic cloves, finely sliced

½ small red chilli, finely chopped (optional)

1kg squid, cleaned and chopped into quarters

salt, to taste

250g cherry tomatoes, chopped in half

a handful of parsley, roughly chopped

6 tbsp white wine

Heat the olive oil in a saucepan over a high heat. Add the squid and a pinch of salt and fry for 5-6 minutes until tinged with gold.

Turn the heat to medium, then add the anchovies and capers and fry until the anchovies dissolve. At this stage, add the garlic and chilli, if using, and fry for a minute, taking care not to burn.

Tip in the wine and leave to evaporate a little.

Add the cherry tomatoes and parsley, reduce the heat to low, cover with a lid and simmer for 45 minutes, then serve.

Gennaro Contaldo is a chef and TV presenter whose shows include Two Greedy Italians. *He has written several books including* Limoni *and* Gennaro's Cucina

Ken Hom

COMFORTING RICE WITH CHINESE SAUSAGE

My mother was a whirlwind of efficiency and skill in the kitchen. She had to be. She would get up at 5am to walk to work with her Chinese friends and only arrived home at around 5.45pm. There was little time for her to shop, but she had a knack for putting together a handful of ingredients in such an artful way that the result was not only quick and comforting, but always totally delectable. By 7pm we would be enjoying a mini feast of at least four dishes.

This simple rice dish would often be one of them. As the rice was cooking, my mother would lay two or three Chinese sausages on the surface, so their rich, sweet-savoury flavour and aroma dripped slowly into the rice, turning it into something really special. What made it even more brilliant was that my mother would fry eggs to put on top, then drizzle them with oyster sauce. It was heaven on earth. To this day, this is the dish I always make when I am looking for a quick and satisfying meal.

Chinese sausages are made of pork and pork fat marinated in spices, then hung on strings to dry. They can be found at Chinese grocers and supermarkets.

SERVES 4

2 cups long grain white rice
(about 300g)

6 Chinese pork sausages

Put the rice in a heavy-bottomed medium-sized pot. Pour in enough water to cover the rice by about 2.5cm. Bring to a boil and cook until most of the water has evaporated, then reduce the heat to the lowest possible setting, cover tightly and cook for 2 minutes more.

Cut the sausages diagonally into 5cm slices and place on top of the steaming rice. Cover again tightly and continue to cook for 15 minutes. The rice and sausage will cook slowly in the remaining steam. Turn off the heat and let it rest, still covered, for another 15 minutes before serving.

Ken Hom OBE is a Chinese-American chef and author. Through his TV series, books and classes, he has been teaching people how to cook Chinese cuisine for more than 40 years

Caroline Eden

RED LENTIL KOFTAS

I grew up in a small bungalow just outside Reading where the lawn was kept neat and the evenings were Sunday-quiet. The annual highlight for my family was a two-week holiday in Spain which would involve an endless stream of sticky ice-lollies, sea swimming, sizzling plates of paella and dancing at night. We'd anticipate it all summer long. Mum would play Spanish music in the lead up to the big departure and she'd shop for new summer dresses. I'd join in with the preparations, choosing new shoes and sun cream and floppy hats.

We didn't travel further afield, or for longer periods. There wasn't money for ski trips or long-haul travel. Instead, we bolstered our outlook of the world in the sitting rooms of our neighbours. Mum was incredibly vivacious and beautiful and everyone loved her, none more than me, her only child. Our Iranian neighbours, Ibrahim and Parand, who'd cook Mum and Dad rich lamb dishes and gift us sacks of the finest pistachios, became such good friends that my parents took in their two daughters for many months so that they could finish their schooling when their parents had to return to Tehran.

Then there is Irmak, from Istanbul, who still lives just around the corner from my childhood home and who was one of Mum's closest friends. She had two daughters who both had fantastically curly auburn hair, exactly the same as their mother. I befriended the younger one, Elif. A couple of memories still stand out. The first was when I first saw Irmak's bedroom, which had at its centre, right above the bed, a huge wooden framed portrait of the founder of the Turkish Republic, Mustafa Kemal Atatürk, on horseback, in full military uniform, with an army racing behind him. The other memory is how I'd sit with Elif, and her older sister, Aileen, in front of the television, and how together we'd collectively sort through huge plastic tubs of red lentils, checking for any stones or grit. In the kitchen, Irmak would prepare Turkish soups and stews, and there would sometimes be grilled meat in the garden. The smells would waft in – tomato, rice, lamb and barley simmering – and I'd imagine what Turkey might be like, a country I'd grow to love as an adult, and one I'd come to write about.

There is no doubt that these kind neighbours stoked my intense desire to see the wider world. But they also provided me with vital early life lessons: that travelling vicariously has its merits, that it pays to carefully listen to people's stories, and that there is plenty of magic to be found in the ordinary and the everyday.

100g bulgur (cracked wheat)	
200g red lentils	
3 tbsp olive oil	
1 large onion, finely chopped	
2 cloves of garlic, crushed	
2 tbsp tomato purée	
1 tbsp Turkish pepper paste	
1½ tsp ground cumin	
1½ tsp paprika	
pinch of chilli powder	
pinch of brown sugar	
½ tsp salt	
½ tsp freshly ground black pepper	
1 tbsp lemon juice	
1 tsp sumac to serve	

For the garlic yoghurt

200g Greek-style yoghurt

1 large clove of garlic, crushed

Pick over and rinse the red lentils, then add them to a saucepan, pouring over enough boiling water so that they are covered by a couple of centimetres. Simmer until cooked; this should take around 15 minutes – they need to be almost mushy. Remove the lentils from the heat and drain if there is any excess water. Rinse the bulgur, then add this to the lentil pan, stir, put a lid on and let the steam from the lentils cook the bulgur.

Add 2 tbsp of olive oil to a frying pan and fry the onions until soft and translucent, then add all the other ingredients except the lemon juice and sumac. Stir-fry for 3-4 minutes, add to the lentil and bulgur, then stir to combine really well and let it cool completely. Once cool, add the lemon juice. Meanwhile, whisk the yoghurt with the crushed garlic and place in a little serving bowl. Set aside.

Take 1 tbsp of the lentil bulgur mixture into the palm of your hand and roll a walnut-sized ball. Make a little indentation in the middle, then place on the plate you will serve them on. Repeat until the mixture is used up. Drizzle over your remaining olive oil, trying to get a little drop in each indentation. Dust with sumac and serve with the garlicky yoghurt on the side.

Caroline Eden writes about food and travel for The Guardian, FT *and* The Times Literary Supplement; *her latest book,* Red Sands, *follows her food adventures around Central Asia*

Zoe Adjonyoh

CORNED BEEF STEW

This recipe brings back so many memories of my childhood – mostly of the uncommon silence between my sister Natalie and me while we were chomping away eating this. I know many Ghanaians will recall this humble meal from their childhoods. Corned beef is commonly salt-cured brisket of beef; the process involves treating the brisket with large-grained rock salt, also called corns of salt, and sometimes using sugar and spices or honey and mustard. This recipe, you may be relieved to hear, only requires you to buy a tin of canned corned beef – though feel free to buy corned beef from the butcher or try curing your own.

Corned beef is an ingredient common to both my Irish and my Ghanaian culinary roots, and it's a dish that has surprised a lot of people who aren't used to tinned meat. It was a favourite for my mum, because it was dinner in 30 minutes; for me, it's a childhood favourite that brings a heady nostalgia for the early 1980s. It's also responsible for my career in food, as the recipe gave me my first "cooking lesson" from my father when I was about eight years old.

My dad's kitchen outfits were mostly top-off numbers matched with loose jeans; skinny chested, tightly curled hairs springing wildly, he strode the full length of the kitchen in two steps, Otis or Bob blasting from the subwoofers in the living room. I was standing to one side of the hob while I watched him prepare the chale sauce – a sort of Ghanaian passata – that made it into everything he cooked, from okra soup to jollof sauce and groundnut stew.

Once the simple spiced tomato base was whizzed up, the rest was pretty simple. Some eggs would be put on to be hard boiled – so hard that the pan would almost cook dry if I didn't rescue them. Then his very roughly chopped onions would be sautéed until a little over-caramelised for my tastes now – nearly burnt was Dad's MO – and the spices furiously mixed with the onions. Cooking wasn't a slow process for Dad; it was in a hurry with one goal: sustenance. Apart from carefully dividing the corned beef into eight equal pieces, no attention was paid. Smoke and scorch would rise from the pan, the splash-back was as speckled as an impressionist painting. "How do you know when it's done Dad?" I asked coyly, wanting to save my corned beef from disintegration. "When it is up on the back of the cooker it is done," he laughed. I turned off the hob, pleased with the feast before me.

SERVES 2-4

For the chale sauce

200g canned or 300g
  fresh tomatoes

1 red bell pepper, roasted

2 garlic cloves (optional)

1 tbsp tomato purée

1 small white onion,
  roughly diced

2-3cm piece fresh root ginger,
  grated

½ tsp dry chilli flakes

½ tsp chilli powder

1 tsp extra-hot Madras curry
  powder

½ small Scotch bonnet
  de-seeded or ½ tsp cayenne

salt, to taste

For the stew

300ml chale sauce (as above)

1 x 340g tin corned beef, divided
  into 4-6 pieces

1 medium onion, finely diced

1 tsp extra hot chilli powder

1 tsp curry powder

1 tbsp tomato purée

100ml vegetable stock

2 carrots, finely diced

75g frozen peas (optional)

4 boiled eggs

2 tbsp cooking oil, to fry

To make the chale sauce, blend all the ingredients to a smooth consistency.

To make the stew, heat the oil and sauté the onion over a medium heat until it starts to gently brown and caramelise. Add the dry spices and combine – then add the tomato purée and cook together for 1-2 minutes until it deepens in colour to a sort of brick red. Use 50ml of the stock to deglaze the pan – allow the liquid to evaporate a little before adding the carrots. Once the carrots soften (2-3 minutes), add the remaining stock.

When the liquid has reduced by half, add the chale sauce and reduce heat to medium-low for 15 minutes. Gently place the delicate corned beef pieces into the pan and add the whole boiled eggs; over the next 5-8 minutes gently turn the beef and the eggs so all sides are coated with the stew. Add the peas if using and let simmer for a few minutes until cooked through.

Serve with fluffy boiled yams and dodo (sweet fried plantain) or over rice – either way it will vanish in no time!

Zoe Adjonyoh is a chef and founder of pop-up restaurant Zoe's Ghana Kitchen, which is also the title of her cookbook

Nigella Lawson

MY MOTHER'S PRAISED CHICKEN

My Mother's Praised Chicken is not so much a recipe as my family's culinary fingerprint, the dish that says "Home" to me. And since my mother died so long before my children were born, by making it I feel they are getting to eat her food. The chicken itself is not quite poached, not quite braised, and so I settled on "praised" which feels exactly right, as for me both cooking and eating it feel like a devotional act.

Having said that, I don't feel restricted to making it exactly as she did and nor do I expect you to. This is essentially part of that canon of free-form cooking that a recipe seems to argue against. So please feel free to improvise, adding ginger and chillies, replacing the vermouth or dry white wine with sake or Shaoxing wine (or leaving it out altogether) as wished. And while it's eaten with rice in my family, there is no reason you have to follow suit. And finally, yes, it is drably unphotogenic, but the delicious comfort it delivers is profound.

SERVES 4-8

- 1 large chicken (preferably organic)
- 2 tsp garlic-infused olive oil
- 100ml white wine
- 2-3 leeks, cleaned, trimmed and cut into 7cm logs
- 2-3 carrots, peeled and cut into batons
- 1-2 sticks celery, sliced
- about 2 litres cold water
- 1 bouquet garni (or 1 tsp dried herbs)
- 1 small bunch fresh parsley
- 2 tsp sea salt
- 2 tsp red peppercorns (or 2 tsp of good grinding pepper)
- English mustard
- fresh dill, chopped

Get out a large, flame-safe cooking pot (with a lid) in which the chicken can fit snugly: mine is 28cm wide x 10cm deep.

On a washable board, untruss the chicken, put it breast-side down and press down until you hear the breastbone crack. (As you may imagine, I like this.) Then press down again, so that the chicken is flattened slightly. Now cut off the ankle joints below the drumstick (but keep them); I find kitchen scissors up to the task.

Put the oil in the pan to heat, then brown the chicken for a few minutes breast-side down. Turn up the heat and turn over the chicken, tossing in the feet as you do so. Add the wine or vermouth to the pan and let it bubble down a little before adding the leeks, carrots and celery.

Pour in enough cold water to cover the chicken, though the very top of it may poke out, then pop in the bouquet garni or your herbs of choice, and the parsley stalks (if I have a bunch, I cut the stalks off to use here, but leave them tied in the rubber band) or parsley sprigs.

Bring to a bubble, clamp on the lid, turn the heat to very low and leave to cook for 1½-2 hours. I tend to give it 1½ hours, then leave it to stand with the heat off but the lid still on for the remaining 20-30 minutes.

Nigella Lawson is a cook, broadcaster and food writer. She has written several best-selling cookbooks including Cook, Eat and Repeat

Angel Zapata Martin

MIGAS WITH CHORIZO, PORK BELLY AND BLACK PUDDING

My parents were a busy couple with full-time jobs in Barcelona and during the school holidays I would often spend time at my grandparents' house in Martorell. This was a country area about an hour's drive from town and I loved it there. Everything was different.

Days started early and at dawn my grandfather would be out in the garden, tending his fruit and vegetables. I would watch him through the misty glass of my bedroom window, then come downstairs to find my grandma, Isabel, sitting by the fire making migas.

This simple, country dish, made with stale bread (*ogaza*), chorizo, onion, black pudding, slices of pork belly, long green peppers and lots of fried garlic, was originally intended to set people up for long, cold days out in the fields – and, in my grandfather's case, it still did. For me, though, it always seemed like a feast, something splendid and magnificent.

The bread needed soaking the night before, and my grandmother would cut it into thin slices, sprinkle them with water and put them in a big plastic container, covered with a tea towel, in readiness for the morning. It felt like a kind of ritual. There was no proper kitchen or gas, just the fireplace with its big black *caldero*, filled with hot oil. My grandmother would line the ingredients up on a table next to her and fry them in batches – first the chorizo, then the black pudding and so on – until it was perfectly caramelised. Then she would stir the moistened pieces of bread through the richly flavoured oil until they turned crisp and golden. When the crumbs were ready, the other ingredients were arranged around them in the pan, and the dish placed in the middle of the table.

My grandma would serve her migas outside and there were always people who popped in to help eat it – family, friends, neighbours – everyone digging in with their spoons, straight from the *caldero*. It was an amazing experience, not just the flavour of the fried *ogaza*, mixed with fatty chorizo, black pudding and pork belly, which was incredible, but the setting – sitting in the open air among the abundance of my grandfather's garden. It is a moment I'll never forget.

SERVES 4

1 loaf white sourdough or other rustic white bread, at least 2-3 days old (you want it to be dry and hard)

1 head of garlic, divided into cloves with their skin on

4 long green peppers (friggitello)

4 large fresh sardines

2 morcilla de cebolla (onion black puddings), halved

2 spicy cooking chorizo, about 110g each, halved

500g pork belly, cut into 4 steaks

500g grapes

olive oil

The night before you are going to make the migas, cut the bread into thin slices. It is important that they are as similar in size as possible. Dip your fingers in water and sprinkle the bread gently – but it shouldn't be wet, or it will ruin the dish. Leave overnight in a plastic bowl covered with a clean tea towel.

Next day, heat a caldero or heavy cast-iron casserole pan over a medium-high heat. Add a generous quantity of olive oil and fry all the meats and garnishes individually until they are cooked. Do this steadily and in batches, leaving the same oil in the pan throughout. Start with the garlic, then the peppers, sardines, morcilla, chorizo and pork belly. When each ingredient has been fried, remove from the pan and put to one side.

Next, add the soaked crumbs to the same hot oil. It will spit a bit but that's OK. Turn down the heat and continue cooking, stirring gently, for about 15-20 minutes. After 5 minutes, add the fried garlic and a pinch of salt. You want to end up with big crumbs of bread that are crunchy and golden outside, but still soft and spongy inside. Taste and adjust the seasoning with salt and pepper if needed.

Arrange the sausages, pork cuts, sardines and peppers around the migas in the caldero. Scatter with the grapes and serve straight from the pan, with guests sitting around the table with their own spoon. Don't forget the red wine.

Angel Zapata Martin was the executive chef of London's Barrafina restaurants and Parrillan

Angela Hartnett

SPINACH AND RICOTTA TORTELLI

I always remember cooking with Nonna. As her eldest granddaughter, I was expected to help in the kitchen and, though it sometimes felt like a chore, secretly I loved it. There was no such expectation of my brother, of course, even though he was two years older than me.

At particular times of year, Nonna and I would make pasta together: spinach and ricotta tortelli at Easter and anolini at Christmas. Nonna did everything by hand, even when she was 80-plus, and by the time we were done my little arms would be exhausted from kneading. Part of me just wanted to be with my mates or watching *Grange Hill*, so when it came to spacing out the filling on the rolled sheets of pasta, I would make the blobs as big as possible to try and get the job done more quickly. It never worked. Eagle-eyed Nonna would go along behind me and make them smaller again. She was right, of course – the pasta is just as important as the filling.

Once we'd finish making them, I would count the pieces and freeze them to share out among the family or to keep for when we were all together on Easter Sunday or Christmas Day. Afterwards, Nonna and I would sit and eat together. Sometimes, we would turn the trimmings into fresh tagliatelle, served with Nonna's meat ragu. Sometimes, we would try out the pasta we had made, adding just melted butter and Parmesan. We always ate at the table, never in front of the TV.

They were happy times. Just Nonna and me – and a plate of delicious food.

SERVES 4

For the pasta

200g 00 flour

2 whole eggs

For the filling

400g spinach, blanched

150g ricotta

pinch nutmeg, grated

75g Parmesan, grated

pinch of pepper, freshly milled

1 egg, beaten

semolina flour

To serve

50g butter

8 fresh sage leaves

Parmesan, grated

For the filling: thoroughly squeeze the spinach to remove as much moisture as possible, then chop it finely. Place in a bowl with the ricotta and remaining filling ingredients, apart from the beaten egg and semolina flour, mix thoroughly and season to taste. Place the mixture in a piping bag and refrigerate until ready to use.

For the pasta: tip the flour onto the work surface and make a hole in the centre. Add the eggs to the hole and mix lightly. Gradually stir the eggs with your hands, drawing in flour as you go. Continue until the flour and eggs have come together to form a dough. Continue to knead until the dough is a smooth ball. This should take at least 5 minutes. Cover with cling film and leave to rest for a minimum of 30 minutes.

Cut your pasta dough in half. Leave one half in clingfilm. With the other half, roll thinly onto a floured surface with a rolling pin. Set the rollers of your pasta machine to the maximum width and roll the pasta through twice, ensuring the pasta remains at the full width of the machine. Continue this process, but each time taking the setting down by one notch until the pasta is approximately 2mm thick.

Lay the pasta out on a floured surface and trim the edges. Pipe walnut-sized amounts of spinach filling just inside the pasta edge nearest to you. Egg-wash the edge furthest from you and in between the mounds of filling.

Fold the pasta over once, pressing around the filling to ensure any air is removed. Fold again, sealing the pasta on the final turn. Cut with a serrated pasta cutter and place onto a tray with semolina flour.

Bring a pan of salted water to the boil. Add the pasta and cook for 3 minutes.

Meanwhile, melt the butter in a pan, add the sage and cook for a few minutes. Drain the pasta, put it in a serving dish and serve with the sage butter, Parmesan and black pepper.

Angela Harnett MBE is chef patron of Murano and Café Murano in London and Cucina Angela in Courchevel

William Sitwell

SPAGHETTI CARBONARA

I feel possessive about spaghetti carbonara. It's rather like being on the tube and seeing someone holding a copy of *The Spectator*. I feel that it's mine. It's something I've enjoyed all my life. It's personal. And it's a dish I loved and would cook before the food world enveloped me.

There are many in this industry, be they writers or chefs, who talk about their childhoods, where food and the subject of food was the mainstay of the family. At one meal what would be eaten at the next was the main topic of conversation. I don't come from such a family. My personal struggle was simply to get through mealtimes. No disrespect to my mother, but we were a meat and two veg household: a chop, carrots and mash, prepared as quickly as possible, endured and then finished so the rest of the day could continue. My mother still has a Belling heater where her vegetables rest… no al dente broccoli in her house.

This lack of interest coupled with my lack of appetite meant I was very thin and would have to spend hours staring at cold veg on my plate after everyone had long left the table. I couldn't "get down" until I had finished. It wasn't much fun. But her chocolate cake was – and still is. And today I still relish making the same carbonara as I did then, with no veg or salad in sight.

Now I've been a food writer for several decades I can pronounce on spaghetti carbonara and pontificate that it must be nothing more than pork bits – bacon or lardons – pasta and a raw egg turned in at the end, off the heat. No cream. No garlic. Nothing else, except cracked black pepper and a mountain of Parmesan.

Today, that cheese is better – it's not shaken from a little carton. And I still take pride in cooking the same dish that gave me pleasure when I was "Boneyman", as my father called me. Now, as it calls for a glass of good Chardonnay or Rioja, it's a plate of convivial happiness, a constant loyal companion through the ups and downs of life.

SERVES 2

- 100g spaghetti
- 2 rashers dry-cured unsmoked streaky bacon
- 1 tsp extra virgin olive oil
- 1 large organic egg
- 1 tbsp freshly grated Parmigiano Reggiano, plus extra to serve

Bring a large pan of salted water to the boil. Cook the spaghetti according to the pack instructions. Drain, keeping back 2 tablespoons of the cooking water.

Meanwhile, cut the bacon rashers into 1cm pieces. Warm a frying pan over a high heat, then add the olive oil and bacon. Cook for 3-4 minutes until crisp.

Add the drained pasta to the frying pan. Remove from the heat and crack the egg into the pan. Stir well to coat the pasta, adding the 1 tablespoon of cheese and the reserved cooking water as you mix. Season with freshly ground black pepper. Serve on a warm plate with extra black pepper and the extra cheese grated over.

William Sitwell is restaurant critic for **The Telegraph** *and founder of William's House Wines, the world's smallest wine store*

Mike Robinson

WILD RABBIT KORMA

My mother didn't get time to cook much. To be honest, I don't think it was her favourite pastime and she fully embraced the convenience of the ready-meal culture that came in little neat packets from Marks & Spencer. The family favourite was chicken korma, which became our staple and we never grew tired of it or felt hard done by to see it on our plates yet again.

When I was 12, I decided I wanted to cook my own version from scratch. I found a recipe in a book – there wasn't any internet 40 years ago – went down to the paddock at the bottom of the garden armed with my trusty air rifle and, eventually, succeeded in shooting a rabbit. With the help of my elderly neighbour Archie – a proper old-fashioned countryman who had been through the hardship of the war years – I gutted and skinned it and took it home to cook.

We didn't have all the ingredients, but I managed to cobble something together, which couldn't have been much more than water, onions, rabbit and curry powder. I made rice dyed with turmeric to go with it, as I'd seen in takeaways from the local curry house. My parents told me it was delicious. I don't actually remember how it tasted, but I'm sure it was fairly disgusting. More than anything though, it was one of the first times I remember going out to hunt, gut and skin the food for our table – a way of eating that has stuck with me ever since.

The recipe here is for a rabbit curry that's a lot more palatable – in fact, it's completely delicious. Not everyone can go out and shoot their own rabbit, but you'll find them in a good butcher, especially if you ask.

SERVES 4-6

- 2 wild rabbits, cut into joints, with the saddles cut into 3 pieces
- 2 x 400g cans coconut milk
- ¼ pineapple, peeled and cut into chunks
- 100g butter
- 6 cloves garlic, crushed
- 1 onion, finely diced
- 1 tbsp turmeric
- 2 tbsp garam masala
- 2 medium red chillies, chopped
- 2 limes
- ½ bunch fresh coriander
- salt and pepper

First, put the rabbit pieces in the coconut milk from one of the cans mixed with the pineapple chunks and place in the fridge to marinate (this tenderises the rabbit beautifully).

Pat the rabbit dry and put aside.

Melt the butter in a heavy pan and fry the garlic and onion. When soft, add the turmeric, garam masala and chopped chilli. Cook for 10 minutes on a low heat, then add the rabbit, turning it well and browning it gently. Squeeze in the limes and add the second can of coconut milk and enough water to cover the rabbit. Simmer for 90 minutes, moving the meat around gently. When the rabbit is tender and starting to come off the bone, season to taste and add the chopped coriander. Serve with old-school yellow rice.

Mike Robinson is chef, hunter gatherer and co-owner of the Michelin-starred Harwood Arms in London

SPICED MUTTON STEW

When I was growing up in Meerut in Uttar Pradesh, it was always expected that I would follow in my father's footsteps and train to become a doctor. Much to his disappointment, I tried very hard at this but was unable to make the cut. My father disapproved of my choice to train as a chef instead, and it was my mother who really inspired me to follow this passion.

Ironically, perhaps, she was never a great cook herself. As a teacher, she was often too busy to dedicate time in the kitchen, which earnt her the nickname "the pressure cooker" in our house. From a young age I helped with the cooking at home, often offering to make dinner when my mother didn't have time to. This recipe is a somewhat rare example of a dish that she executed well (without the use of a pressure cooker). It is a firm favourite in my household these days and one that always makes me think of her fondly. Once you've sourced some of the harder-to-find ingredients, it is actually very straightforward and requires minimal effort for most satisfying results.

SERVES 4

1kg boneless mutton leg (or lamb) cut into 2-3cm cubes

1kg Bombay onion or red onion, sliced

650g fresh tomatoes, chopped

70g fresh garlic cloves, chopped

80g fresh ginger, peeled, cut into thin matchsticks

10 dried red Kashmiri chillies

5 black cardamom pods

15 peppercorns

5 medium-sized bay leaves

2-3 cinnamon sticks (around 5cm each)

5g cumin seeds

15g yellow chilli powder, optional (if using, reduce the number of dried chillies)

300g sunflower oil

150g yoghurt

1 level tsp sea salt

small bunch fresh coriander

Place the mutton into a large, heavy-bottomed cooking pot. Cover with cold water, stir, then drain, leaving the meat in the pot. Put 20-30 ginger matchsticks to one side for garnishing. Add the rest to the pot along with the onions, tomato, garlic, chillies, spices and oil, plus 225ml of water. Mix well. Place over a medium-high heat and bring to a simmer, turning the ingredients over regularly until the onions and tomatoes have let out some juice.

Turn the heat down just a little to maintain a lively simmer, add a lid and cook, stirring regularly, for 45-60 minutes or until the onion and tomatoes are reduced to a sauce-like consistency and the mutton cooked through. The meat may tense slightly at the beginning, but will relax to tenderness towards the end of cooking.

Once the meat is tender, remove the lid and increase the heat to a rapid simmer. Add the yoghurt and salt; continue to stir regularly. Cook until the sauce thickens and becomes slightly darker, and oil separates to the top – around 20-30 minutes. Taste for salt, season if necessary.

Finely chop the coriander. Add three-quarters to the pot and stir. Serve in bowls garnished with coriander and ginger matchsticks, with roomali roti or naan.

Naved Nasir is chef director of Dishoom, which has restaurants in London, Birmingham, Manchester and Edinburgh

Vivek Singh

CHINGRI MALAI CURRY

I first had this dish at a wedding feast in North Brook Colliery near Asansol in West Bengal. I was eight years old. The community was a small one and most of the time we would come across the same people at every event or celebration. The menus, too, were more or less the same. Except, that is, in the wedding season, when there would often be more than one wedding on the same date and my parents would need to prioritise. I considered myself the weddings expert and I would often volunteer to represent the family at the events my parents couldn't attend themselves.

Dressed in my best clothes, and clutching a five rupee note in an ornate envelope that read "With Best Wishes and Blessings to the Newlyweds from RP Singh and Family", I would walk up to the podium and hand it to the bride and groom, then make my way to the marquee where food was being served.

I loved attending weddings. I learnt a lot just soaking in the atmosphere and observing. I learnt the importance of organisation, of coordination, of hierarchy and of hospitality, all of it at these weddings. It's not uncommon to invite 1,200 people to a wedding in India, and with those numbers, nobody would blame you if you didn't force people to eat. But in Bengal, it wasn't so. Rows of servers would pass in front of long tables giving people seconds, often thirds of the dozen or more dishes on the menu. Such was the warmth of Bengali hospitality.

The wedding where I first ate this dish was one such feast. It was the first time I had tasted shrimp in my life and it was an unforgettable experience: the rich, fragrant and heady sauce, sweet with fat shrimps bathed in gold. It completely changed my understanding of taste, flavour and fragrance and the memory has stayed with me all my life. It may even be the reason I chose food as a career.

SERVES 2

400g raw prawns, the
    largest you can find, peeled
    and deveined

1 tsp ground turmeric

1 tsp salt

3 tbsp vegetable oil or ghee

2 bay leaves

2 white onions, blended into a
    fine paste

1 tbsp ground cumin

2 tbsp ginger and garlic paste

2 green chillies, slit lengthways

250ml shellfish stock or water

75ml coconut milk

½ tsp sugar

4-5 green cardamom pods,
    ground

1 tbsp chopped coriander

Peel the prawns and marinate for 5 minutes with half the turmeric and half the salt.

Heat half the oil in a pan and add the bay leaves and onion paste. Sauté over a medium heat for 10-12 minutes until very light brown.

Meanwhile, heat the remaining oil in a non-stick frying pan and sear the prawns briefly for 1-2 minutes, turning so they sear on both sides. Set aside.

Mix the turmeric, ground cumin and ginger-garlic paste with 75ml water. Add to the sautéed onions, reduce the heat and cook for 2-3 minutes, stirring regularly.

Add the remaining salt and green chillies and stir for 1 minute, then pour in the stock, mix in the coconut milk and simmer for 2-3 minutes. Add the prawns and cook for a minute or so until they are just cooked, adding a little more stock if necessary.

Correct the seasoning with salt and sugar and sprinkle on the ground cardamom and chopped coriander. Squeeze over the lime juice and serve.

This is best eaten with freshly boiled basmati rice, enriched with a tablespoon of ghee or cold salted butter, a pinch of smoked sea salt and freshly cracked black pepper. Add the butter, salt and pepper to hot steaming rice, mix and serve immediately.

Vivek Singh is a chef and owner of the Cinnamon Club group of restaurants. He has written several cookbooks, including Vivek Singh's Indian Festival Feasts

Valentine Warner

TROUT IN A HEDGE

You wouldn't know I was any relation of the famed cricketer Pelham Warner, or Plum as he was more widely known. My own early accomplishments on the sports field were limited to some remarkably long daisy chains and a dizzying number of own goals. If I was ever passed – and happened to catch – a rugby ball, it was a tactical manoeuvre that allowed me to be justifiably stampeded and trampled. Irritated cries of "Oh no, we've got Warner" and "NOT THAT WAAAAY!" only intensified my dislike of competitive testosterone. So I laid down the bat and ball and took up smoking instead, my only subsequent displays of athletic intent being when I was hotly pursued by teachers or prefects.

As my smoker's safe bushes became "blown and known", I'd wander ever-increasing miles to lie in the summer grass and exhale towards the clouds, my ears filled with the happy sound of bees, rather than "Pass it, Warner, you f***ing idiot". On one such meandering, I noticed a path that slipped away from the road, its verges embroidered with campion, stitchwort, cow parsley and foxgloves. The track led through a field of swishing grasses to a small bridge over a gurgling stream.

To the right of me, on the other side of a padlocked gate, was a series of ponds, each with an aerator splashing a fount of bubbles at one end. I climbed over the Keep Out sign and went in to explore. Releasing the bungee rope and lid from a galvanised bin, I pushed my hand into the brown pellets and strewed them out over the murky water. An eruption of thrashing and boiling confirmed my hopes. I'd struck silver – a trout farm.

With my then best friend beside me, the next three years saw some artful poaching. Most fish we put back, many we kept or gave away. School food being the miserable slop that it was, I'd use the empty sixth-form kitchens to fry trout in cheap butter, laying them upon toasted Mother's Pride and finishing them with dusty pepper. The flip side of such delight was many painful and panicked exits through the trout farm's barbed wire and, if caught, powerful shakings from its employees.

Thirty-one years later, at a food festival in Ibiza, an elegant grey-haired man approached me. "Hi Valentine," he said, "I'm Miles. You put a considerable dent in my profits."

"What are you talking about?" I replied, taken aback.

"That was my trout farm you used to poach from."

"Oh shit," I replied.

"Yes," he continued jovially, "I think you had a fair few, didn't you?"

"To be precise," I replied, "if you find the large alder tree upstream of the bridge, there's a leaping trout carved into the bark with the initials VW and NC and the words '293 fish, 1987-1990'."

"I think the matter could be settled, perhaps, by you coming to cook a gratis private dinner for six at mine," he suggested with a smirk.

"Seems fair enough," I remember replying. "But first let me buy you a glass of rosé for your pains."

SERVES 2

wild garlic, nettle tops and
   Alexanders tops

2 tbsp breadcrumbs

50g coarsely grated butter

1 heaped tsp Dijon mustard

1 tbsp baby capers

a scratch of lemon zest

2 tsp lemon juice

450g trout, gutted and gills
   removed

salt and pepper

1 level tsp sea salt

small bunch fresh coriander

Come April, head out into the hedgerows and woods. Pick a large handful of wild garlic, its buds, a few nettle tops and some Alexanders tops, the latter being optional. (Note: all three are easily identified and can be found in most foraging books.)

Wash these well, dry them thoroughly and chop very finely. Light your barbeque charcoal or turn your grill to full.

Mix the wild greens with the breadcrumbs, butter, mustard, capers, lemon zest and juice, plus a really good grind of pepper and a little salt. Combine together well.

Take the trout and dry its exterior thoroughly. Lay on a board and, taking a very sharp knife, cut from the tail end up, on both sides, releasing the fillets from the spine but still leaving both fillets attached to the head. Cut out the spine at the head end and discard it.

This will leave you with a flapper. Stuff the fish with the hedgerow breadcrumb butter. Tie the fish up with 3 or 4 short lengths of string and cut off the knot ends.

Season the fish well with salt and grill to your preference, hopefully achieving a crispy coloured skin. Accompany with a glass of good rosé.

Valentine Warner is a cook, food writer and broadcaster, as well as co-founder of Hepple Spirits. His books include The Consolation of Food

Yotam Ottolenghi

HOPPEL POPPEL

This is a dish from Berlin, where my mother's father is from, and she used to prepare it when I was growing up. My mother wasn't very particular about the ingredients – it's a great user-up for day-old potatoes and any odd bits of cooked meat – but frankfurters are probably the best. Pork sausages aren't normally found in Jewish homes, but my mother would go out of her way to get some. I guess the German in her was slightly stronger than the Jew. Us kids loved it for the naughtiness, even though we were under strict instructions not to make too much noise about it to our friends, so as not to offend. On a couple of occasions I made this for my own kids, and though there's no wickedness involved, they still wolfed it down happily.

SERVES 4

8 large eggs

2 tbsp double cream

5g chives, cut into 1cm lengths, plus 1 tbsp extra to garnish

40g unsalted butter

2 tbsp olive oil

1 large onion, halved and sliced ¼cm thick

250g cooked waxy potatoes (such as Charlottes), peeled and cut into roughly 2cm cubes

200g frankfurters, sliced at a slight angle ½cm thick

1 green pepper, cut into roughly 1½cm cubes

80g mozzarella block (low-moisture mozzarella), roughly grated

salt and black pepper

Beat together the eggs, cream, chives, half a teaspoon of salt and plenty of pepper and set aside.

Put 30g of the butter and all the oil in a large, non-stick sauté pan over a medium-high heat. Once hot, add the onion and cook, stirring occasionally, for about 6 minutes, until softened and lightly browned.

Add the potato and frankfurters, half a teaspoon of salt and a good grind of pepper and fry until starting to brown and crisp up, stirring occasionally, another 5 minutes. Stir in the green pepper and cook, for about 7 minutes, or until softened and everything is nicely coloured, shaking the pan often.

Turn the heat down to medium and add the last 10g of butter to the pan, swirling to melt. Pour over the egg mixture and sprinkle with the cheese. Cook for about 3 minutes, using a spatula to gently fold over the mixture in a few places, without completely mixing everything together. Sprinkle over the extra chives and serve directly from the pan.

Israeli-born Yotam Ottolenghi is a chef, restaurateur and food writer, whose books include Plenty *and* Ottolenghi Test Kitchen

Fin Spiteri

TUNISIAN BRAISED LAMB

My grandmother's an incredible person. She speaks four languages and tries to call me on Zoom every day. She emigrated from Tunisia with my grandfather more than 40 years ago and still has the most amazing French-Italian accent. They ran a hotel in Kent together when they first arrived in the UK. I think that's why my family has the hospitality bug.

When we were children, she had a house right across from the beach at Bexhill-on-Sea. We loved visiting her there. Most half-terms we would pile into our old Citroen DS for the drive down from London (keeping our fingers crossed that we wouldn't break down on the way – an all too frequent occurrence).

Our arrival was greeted by the smell of her lamb stew simmering on the stove. We would crowd around her kitchen table, sharing the tender lamb and crumbly couscous, swollen with meaty juices, before falling into bed, tired, sated and ready to begin our holiday.

Her heritage was never more pronounced than when she cooked this dish for us and it always makes me think of her. It carries with it the idea of food as family, the importance of sharing a meal to mark an occasion. And, as our short journey came to an end, it was a reminder of where her own had started, many years before.

SERVES 4-6

olive oil

1kg lamb neck, cubed

2 tsp paprika

½ tsp turmeric

½ tsp ground cumin

½ tsp cayenne

big pinch of salt

¾ tsp garlic powder

2 onions, diced

4 carrots, diced

3 cloves of garlic, minced

400ml chicken stock

½ tbsp tomato paste

1 tbsp honey

½ tbsp harissa paste

a glass of red wine

500g couscous, cooked

First marinate the lamb. Mix together the paprika, turmeric, cumin, cayenne, garlic powder and salt with a couple of tablespoons of olive oil and use the mixture to coat the lamb. This should ideally be left in the fridge overnight, but 4-6 hours will suffice if you've left it too late.

Next, heat more olive oil in a large saucepan and add the lamb. Brown the lamb well before removing from the pan and adding the onions, carrots and garlic. Cook for 5 minutes, then add a large glass of red wine and stir well for another 5 minutes.

Add the stock, tomato paste, honey and harissa, then bang the lamb back in and bring to a boil. Reduce the heat and simmer for a couple of hours. The meat will become very tender. When the smell is too much to bear, take it off the heat and serve over the couscous, ideally to a hungry and travel-weary family.

Fin Spiteri is a cocktail consultant and co-founder with his brother Lorcan of Studio Kitchen as well as Caravel, a barge restaurant on the Regent's Canal in London

Lee Tiernan

DEVENNEY CON CARNE ON JACKET SPUDS

I was a terrible eater as a kid. I had very little interest in real food or, according to my mum, any desire to engage in eating at all. I remember a feeling of revulsion when confronted with a forkful of food. It was a battle of wills. I cradled a conscious, genuine empathy for her predicament – I just didn't want to participate. In a bid to infuse her young son with vital vitamins, my mother, Moira, became an expert at sneaking fruit and vegetables into my daily diet, a tactic I now employ with my own children. Disguising spinach in smoothies and puréed vegetables in pasta sauces is way easier than trying to persuade them to eat something they identify as yucky.

I was chatting to my mum about this when she mentioned that the chilli con carne I gradually grew to love was about 50 per cent mashed and finely chopped vegetables, combined with beef mince and tomato sauce. There are so many variations of chilli, I don't know what authentic chilli con carne is, and I'm pretty sure my mum didn't either back in 1986, especially when it was served on a jacket potato with melted Cheddar on top. I will always trade flavour for authenticity anyway, so it's a moot point in my eyes.

Listening to my mum describe the process, I decided to recreate her chilli for this book. I've tinkered with the spices to amplify the flavour and added coriander and spring onion to the jacket spud. You can supplement any veg, by the way.

I recommend eating this on a Sunday afternoon while watching *Antiques Road Show*, after riding round all day on your Raleigh Burner BMX with your mates.

SERVES 6, generously

- 6 large baking potatoes
- 1 medium aubergine
- 4-5 flat field mushrooms
- 5-6 cloves of garlic
- 1 medium-large onion
- 500g of the best quality beef mince you can buy
- 1 x 400g tin of chopped tomatoes
- 6 tbsp tomato purée (about half a tube)
- 3 tbsp ground cumin
- 3 tbsp ground coriander
- Tabasco sauce, to taste

I'm pretty confident most of you know how to bake a potato to your liking. It's a very simple process. Turn your oven on full whack. Wash your spuds. Cut a 1cm deep line around each spud, stab it with a sharp knife or spike a few times, then place on the rack of your oven and bake till dark and crispy on the outside with a soft inside. The size of your potatoes and the efficiency of your oven will determine the cooking time, but allow a good hour. When a skewer goes through with ease, your spud is done.

While your spuds are baking, dice or chop your veg nice and small. You can pulse the veg in a food processor if you're feeling lazy, just don't blitz it too much; we are looking for a bit of texture.

Take a deep frying pan or appropriately-sized pot and place over a medium heat. Add a good glug of neutral oil, such as sunflower or rapeseed (never extra virgin

200ml of IPA or Craft Beer
(you will have to drink the rest
of the can)

3 tbsp Bisto gravy granules

400g tin red kidney beans,
drained and rinsed

juice of ½-1 lime

80g butter, at room
temperature

20g bunch coriander

3-4 spring onions

200g grated mozzarella and
Cheddar, mixed

salt and pepper

olive oil), allow the oil to get up to temperature and dump in all the veg, along with 2 teaspoons of salt. Stir together, then sweat the veg mix until it is translucent. A touch of colour won't hurt.

Add the beef and spices, mix in, then cook for about 5 minutes. I don't worry too much about browning mince for this; if it's good quality with a high fat content, the flavour will come through.

Next squeeze in the tomato purée and pour in the tinned tomatoes followed by the IPA. Stir together, then add the Bisto granules, which will thicken and season the chilli.

Hit the chilli with a few dashes of Tabasco for heat, acidity and seasoning, then finish with the lime juice and the kidney beans. Leave to simmer over a low heat until ready to serve.

When your spuds are baked to perfection, take them out of the oven. If you have a grill function in your oven turn it as high as it will go now; failing that leave your oven on the highest setting to finish the dish. Allow the potatoes to cool for a few minutes. Find the line around the middle of each potato, insert your knife and cut the potatoes in half.

Scoop the middles out of the crispy skins and into a bowl (it goes without saying that you keep the skins). Add the butter to the potato flesh and mix in with a fork until smooth. Chop the coriander and slice the spring onion, then mix into the waiting potato. Season with salt and pepper to taste. Now reload the skins with the mashed spud.

Place your loaded spud halves in a roasting tray, spoon lashings of chilli on top of each half and pile with cheese. Place a few inches from the grill and bake until the cheese is mottled with golden brown spots. Allow to cool for a spell before consuming. This will save you from burning your mouth and rendering your tastebuds useless.

Lee Tiernan was head chef at St John Bread and Wine and now runs FKABAM (Formerly Known as Black Axe Mangal) in London

Alastair Little

COCK-A-LEEKIE

My mother was a pretty formidable cook, with a repertoire incorporating her mother's (an even more accomplished cook) recipes and dishes she had enjoyed on her very extensive travels. She was surely the first person to serve dishes such as gazpacho, fondue bourguignonne or Panang prawn curry in north-east Lancashire in the early 1960s.

Cock-a-leekie was a regular visitor to our dining table for two good reasons: firstly, the availability of very good free-range chickens from a local farm; and secondly, because it was the only way she could get my father to eat chicken.

Mother used to serve it as a soup and I loved it, only much later discovering it was originally a hearty meal in its own right and that it should incorporate prunes. This revelation came in the 1970s on a tube train bound for Parsons Green and reading a newly purchased copy of Jane Grigson's book *Good Things* with its amazing apologia for prunes.

Cock-a-leekie is an ancient dish with a multi-national pedigree. The mythology is that the Auld Alliance between Scotland and France allowed many Scottish noblemen to serve in the French army, almost invariably at war with England, and to be rewarded with titles and estates in France, in particular in Gascony where they acquired a taste for French cooking.

One of the French kings they served was Henri IV whose charitable, stated desire to put a chicken in the pot of every French household on a Sunday had elevated the simple *poule au pot* to the status of a national icon. These Scottish warrior barons and French soldiers seeking opportunities for promotion and plunder took this dish to Scotland, complete with its Agen prunes, and there it stayed.

This is all probably nonsense, but it makes for a nice back story and glamorises my mother's simple but slightly labour-intensive dish. Here is a recipe for it, filtered through 50 years of time and adapted by my own attempts to reproduce it.

SERVES 6

1 x 2kg free-range chicken

1 bouquet garni, consisting of a celery stalk, 2 bay leaves, a sprig each of thyme, rosemary and sage

2 tsp salt

½ tsp white pepper

100g diced celery heart (keep any trimmings)

Boil 3 litres of water in a stockpot deep enough to allow the chicken to be immersed in it. The chicken should fit relatively snugly. Wash the reserved vegetable trimmings, chop coarsely and arrange in the bottom of the stockpot. Place the chicken on top. Pour boiling water over it, add the bouquet garni and salt and pepper. Make sure the chicken is submerged; you may need to place a smaller pan lid or plate on it to achieve this. Bring the pot to a low boil, then turn to a simmer.

After 1 hour, remove the pot from the stove and carefully ladle or pour out as much of the broth as you safely can into a large bowl or pan, without tipping out

500g carrots, trimmed, peeled
    and cut into ½cm rounds
    (keep the trimmings)

2kg small waxy potatoes, peeled
    and cut into 1cm rounds

2kg leeks, trimmed thoroughly,
    and cut into 2cm rounds (keep
    the trimmings)

18 Agen prunes with their
    stones (not pitted)

the chicken or scalding yourself. Remove the chicken, being careful to avoid the hot liquid pouring out of the bird's body cavity. A utensil called a spider, for obvious reasons, is the ideal tool for this and something all kitchens should have. Set the chicken aside to cool while you cook the vegetables in the broth.

Place the leek rounds in a colander and then in a bowl of hot water and stir gently to get rid of any sand or mud. Leave to soak for a few minutes before draining.

Pour the broth remaining in the pan through a sieve and add it to the reserved batch. Wash out the stock pot and return all the liquid to it. Bring to a slow boil, skim thoroughly and add the celery and carrots. After 10 minutes, add the potatoes and after a further 10 minutes the leeks and prunes. Simmer until the vegetables are tender. Taste the broth for seasoning and adjust if required.

To serve you will need a deep ovenproof serving dish big enough to hold the chicken, vegetables and a litre or so of broth. Carefully remove the meat from the chicken and cut into large bite-sized chunks. I leave the drumsticks and wings intact. Arrange this meat in the centre of your dish and then the cooked vegetables around it, taking care to try and keep the prunes intact. Ladle over a litre of the broth. Cover loosely with aluminium foil and warm in a 150C/130C Fan/Gas 2 oven for 15 minutes or so.

Serve in soup plates and season with sea salt and coarse pepper. The bones and remaining broth can make a fine soup in their own right for another winter's day.

The late, great Alastair Little was a chef and food writer who founded his eponymous London restaurant in the 1980s, and more recently Et Al in Sydney

Andy Harris

OCTOPUS STIFADO

I have been going to Greece since the late 1960s, when my parents built a villa perched on a cliff-top on the island of Skiathos in the Sporades. Every summer, we would pack up the estate car, loading it with jars of Marmite and marmalade, tins of butter and ham – what then seemed to be necessities for our survival – and set off on an adventurous journey across Europe.

My earliest memories of island life are of beach tavernas and of falling asleep at the table while my parents and newfound Greek friends ate endless plates of mezedes and drank the night away. Most of my days were spent underwater, collecting sea urchins and *pinnas* (fan mussels), and searching under rocks for octopus or a glimpse of the elusive *rophos* (grouper), one of the most prized fish in the Aegean. When I was 14, I was allowed to fish with a spear and would run triumphantly from the beach, throwing my catch on the kitchen table for my mother to deal with. She would enlist the help of a neighbouring farmer's wife, who would send me back to the rocks to beat the writhing octopus a hundred times to tenderise it. She taught us how to cook octopus every which way. This simple stew still remains a favourite taste and memory of Greece.

SERVES 4

1 octopus (about 1.2kg)

3-4 bay leaves

6 tbsp red wine vinegar

3 tbsp extra virgin olive oil

1 medium onion, peeled and sliced

16 medium Roscoff onions or shallots, peeled and left whole

2 garlic cloves, peeled and thinly sliced

1 tsp coriander seeds, crushed

1 cinnamon stick

2 tbsp flat-leafed parsley, including the stems, finely chopped

1 x 400g tin peeled tomatoes or 2 large ripe tomatoes, roughly chopped

1 tbsp tomato purée

200ml dry red wine

Place the octopus, bay leaves and half the vinegar in a heavy-based saucepan over a medium heat. Bring to the boil, then lower the heat and simmer, covered, for about 45 minutes. Stir occasionally, making sure there's enough liquid in the pan so the octopus doesn't stick.

Transfer the octopus and liquid into a bowl, allow to cool then slice each tentacle into chunks.

In the same saucepan, heat the olive oil over a medium heat and sauté the coriander seeds, cinnamon, parsley, onion, garlic and baby onions or shallots, stirring regularly, for 5 minutes until softened. Add the sliced octopus and liquid, together with the tinned or fresh tomatoes, tomato purée and red wine. Stir well and bring the mixture back to the boil. Season generously with sea salt and freshly ground black pepper and add the remaining vinegar.

Lower the heat and cook, stirring occasionally, for about 20-30 minutes or until the baby onions are tender and the sauce has thickened.

Serve with boiled orzo or short pasta

Andy Harris is a food writer, owner of The Vinegar Shed, which sells rare vinegars and spices, and founder of the Ealing Deli

Barny Haughton

RISOTTO MILANESE

The first real risotto I had was in a restaurant a street or two away from the central train station in Milan. I was 14 years old and on my way back to London after a holiday at our Italian cousin's house near Venice. I was being driven to Milan by a friend of our cousin in her ancient Mini. Every so often the car would overheat and we would stop at a roadside bar to let the engine cool down. I would go into the bar, buy bottled water, and Faith and I would stand and drink it in the shade, watching the lorries thundering past in the heat. The journey took seven hours. We arrived at Milan central station in the late afternoon.

We unloaded the suitcases and bags from the car and carried them up onto the concourse steps, which overlooked the Piazza Duca d'Aosta. I sat with them while Faith drove the car away. A little later, she returned on foot and sat down next to me and held my hand. We were both wearing espadrilles. The piazza dazzled white in the late afternoon sun. I didn't want to go home.

"Shall we go and eat something?" Faith asked. And so we walked to a restaurant just a few minutes away from the station to have supper before catching the night train to London.

I went back to Milan a few years ago, sat on those same steps and looked down at the new modern piazza and the traffic. I searched for the restaurant, too, with my clear memory of walking into its cool interior, of the old black-and-white photographs on the walls, of the table we sat at and the bare white tablecloth, which was only laid after we sat down.

I never did find the restaurant again. But the memory of the risotto returns to me from time to time, like a guardian angel of endings and beginnings, of sadness and happiness. The rice, creamy yet firm, was an almost sunflower yellow, its rich savouriness beyond anything I had ever tasted. And the little silver dish of grated Parmesan – it felt like coming home.

SERVES 4

2 x 5cm pieces of bone marrow

60g butter

olive oil

1 small onion, very finely diced

300g carnaroli or arborio rice

1 small glass dry white wine or
 dry vermouth

1 tsp (about 10 strands) saffron,
 soaked in 1 tbsp warm stock

30-50g Parmesan

1.3 litres veal or chicken stock
 (or a mix of the two), kept
 warm on the stove

Start by roasting the marrow bones. Preheat the oven to 180C/160C Fan/Gas 4. Season the bones well with salt and pepper, cover with foil and roast in the oven for 25 minutes or until the marrow fat has turned to a jellyish consistency. Leave to cool a little, then scoop out the marrow fat with the handle of a teaspoon. Give the bone to your dog, reserving the marrowfat for the risotto.

To make the risotto: heat half the butter in a heavy-based pan with a glug of olive oil, add the onion and cook gently for 6-8 minutes until soft, but not coloured. Turn up the heat to medium, add the rice and stir for 2 minutes, until well coated in butter. Finely chop the bone marrow – you'll need 2 tablespoons – and stir into the onions. Leave to melt for 3 minutes.

Add the wine and the saffron infusion and simmer until this has been absorbed into the rice, then add a ladleful of stock. Continue to add the stock at intervals in this way, stirring all the time, and waiting until the liquid has been absorbed.

When the risotto is cooked – maybe 25 minutes later or even longer, it should be tender but just a little al dente and the mixture should be slightly runny. (Simon Hopkinson says it should collapse gently when you are putting it onto the plate. I agree.)

Never be scared to add a splash more stock if you think it needs it. Remove from the heat, mix in the remaining butter and the Parmesan and season with salt and freshly ground black pepper. Leave to sit for 5 minutes. Serve immediately, with extra Parmesan if you like.

Barny Haughton MBE is a chef and former restaurateur. He now runs the Square Food Foundation, a cookery school and community kitchen that works to reduce hunger, improve health and bring people together through cooking and food

Gizzi Erskine

CHICKEN IN WEEDS

The first incarnation of "Chicken in Weeds" appeared in my very first book, *Kitchen Magic*. It's a curry that my mother adapted from a Madhur Jaffrey recipe from the 1990s, a simple, delicately spiced curry, and I renamed it "Chicken in Weeds" due to the fact that the chicken swam in a pool of coriander.

I still make it regularly at home, though it has developed into what feels like a very different incarnation, superior in its flavour and viscosity. The chicken is more authentically chopped: I use the whole bird, jointed, making for a richer stock, and cook it low and slow so the meat falls off the bone (you can use leg and thigh pieces if you prefer, but I want you to try breaking up a whole chicken) and I've upped the spicing too, including cardamom, turmeric, cloves and cinnamon. I've also made it greener with added spinach, and cashews for a gentle, creamy roundness.

It's completely inauthentic, yet somehow tastes like a curry that should sit among the classics. It makes the most brilliant everyday meal, but also a terrific dish as part of an Indian or Middle Eastern dinner party. My mum was famous for making huge feasts and would serve this with yellow pea tarka dhal and often a beetroot and coconut curry or raw carrot raita.

6 tbsp vegetable oil

1 chicken, skinned and joined (or 6 thigh, leg and wing pieces)

1 onion, roughly chopped

1 head of garlic, cloves peeled and roughly chopped

5cm piece of fresh ginger, peeled and roughly chopped

2 tsp ground cumin

1 tbsp ground coriander

2 green cardamom pods

pinch of ground cloves

½ tsp Kashmiri chilli powder

½ tsp cayenne

½ tsp ground turmeric

500ml fresh chicken stock

1 cinnamon stick

1 green chilli, kept whole

100g coriander, leaves and stalks

100g unsalted cashews

200g spinach leaves, washed

juice of ½ lemon

1 tsp sea salt

cooked basmati rice, to serve

Heat 2 tablespoons of the oil in a casserole dish over a high heat, then brown the chicken pieces in two batches until they are caramelised all over (you may need to add a little more oil to the pan for the second batch of chicken). Remove and set aside.

Add the rest of the oil to the pan, set the heat to medium-low and throw in the onions, garlic and ginger (it will be blitzed to a paste, so don't worry about chopping everything finely). Sweat for at least 20 minutes, until the onions are really soft and golden and have begun to caramelise, then add all of the spices to the dish, except the cinnamon stick and green chilli, and fry for a minute or two before adding the chicken stock. Return the chicken and any residual juices to the dish and add the cinnamon stick and whole green chilli. Cover and cook over a low heat for 40 minutes, until the chicken is starting to come away from the bone.

Remove the chicken from the sauce once more and set aside. Carefully transfer the sauce to a food processor, removing the cardamom pods and cinnamon stick, but including the whole chilli (don't worry about removing the stalk). Add the coriander, cashews and spinach and blitz until smooth – you want everything to be mulched and blended together well. Return this vibrant green sauce to the casserole dish and put the chicken back in. Heat together for 5 minutes but no longer, as you don't want to lose the bright colour of the sauce. Squeeze in the lemon juice and season with the salt. Serve with basmati rice.

Gizzi Erskine is a chef, television presenter and award-winning cookery writer whose books include Restore: Over 100 New, Delicious, Ethical and Seasonal Recipes That are Good For You and For the Planet

Rick Stein

CORNISH BOUILLABAISSE WITH MASH

I must have been nine or 10 at the time. My parents took me, my brother John and my sister Henrietta to have lunch with some friends of theirs at Church Cove on the Lizard Peninsula in Cornwall. Tony Arnell was a famous pianist – this was in the 1950s – and his wife Colette was the daughter of an artist friend of ours, Enslin Du Plessis, who my parents had shared a flat with in Mecklenburgh Square in Bloomsbury. Their daughter Claudine was the absolute centre of my teenage brother's attention and even I couldn't see much difference between her and Brigitte Bardot, who John had photos of in his chest of drawers.

I always assumed that Colette was French, though the family were in fact South African. That didn't stop her from knowing exactly how to cook bouillabaisse. It included saffron, of course, which probably came from Cornwall, but heaven knows where the olive oil came from in those days, or even the garlic – London, I suppose.

Colette made the bouillabaisse with the fish that my dad and I caught off the rocks that morning – bass, wrasse and pollock as far as I can remember. It was one of my earliest memories of foreign cooking and I loved it. I tried to recreate it from memory for a recent TV series. This is the recipe.

SERVES 4

For the mash

1kg potatoes, peeled and cut into
    quarters

pinch saffron

2 tsp salt

150ml full fat milk or cream

50g butter

For the bouillabaisse

5 tbsp olive oil

1 small fennel bulb, chopped

2 strips of orange peel

2 shallots or 1 onion, chopped,
    skin and all

3 cloves garlic, roughly chopped,
    skin and all

100ml dry white wine

600ml water or fish stock

2 large tomatoes, roughly
    chopped

1 tbsp tomato purée

pinch of saffron

pinch of cayenne pepper

salt and pepper

2 whole gurnard, about 600g
    total weight, filleted (ask for the
    head and bones if the filleting is
    done by the fishmonger)

250g Falmouth Bay prawns,
    shell-on (or 6 or so cooked
    langoustines, cut in half
    lengthways)

12 mussels in the shell

For the mash, boil the potatoes in salted water for about 20-25 minutes until tender when prodded with a knife. Drain well and wait for the steam to die down so that the potatoes are fairly dry. Mash the potatoes by either pushing them through a potato ricer, whisking with an electric whisk or using a masher.

While the potatoes are cooking, warm the milk or cream in a small pan with the saffron and butter. When hot, turn off the heat and leave the saffron to infuse the milk. When the potatoes are mashed, beat in the liquid until light and smooth. Whisking the mash with a handheld whisk, such as you'd use to make a cake, gives a wonderfully light whipped texture with no lumps.

Heat the olive oil in a fairly deep, wide pan and fry the shallots, garlic, fennel and gurnard heads and bones until soft. Add the white wine, water or fish stock, tomatoes, tomato purée, orange peel and saffron. Bring to a boil, turn down to a simmer and cook for 30-40 minutes.

Working quickly, push the soup mixture through a sieve with a wooden spoon or the back of a ladle, or pass through a mouli to extract as much flavour as possible from the fish bones and vegetables. Discard the solids.

Rinse the pan and return the soup to the pan to heat through, seasoning to taste with salt, pepper and cayenne. Add the gurnard fillets and prawns and cook for 2 minutes, then add the mussels and cook for a further 2-3 minutes until the mussels have opened.

Spoon some mashed potato onto each warmed plate, top with some of the fish, prawns and mussels, and spoon over a little of the sauce. Serve immediately.

Rick Stein CBE is a chef, broadcaster and owner of The Seafood Restaurant in Padstow, Cornwall and several other restaurants and cafés in Cornwall and around the UK. He is the author of more than 20 books, including his latest, Rick Stein at Home

Sabrina Ghayour

MINCED BEEF AND ONION CRISPY PANCAKES

Food snobs may be shocked to hear that Findus Crispy Pancakes were my all-time favourite 1980s treat. Forget fish fingers and frozen burgers: I could happily have eaten a four-pack of minced beef crispy pancakes every night of the week and never tire of them. As a child of the 1970s and 1980s, I witnessed the era that gave birth to much of the convenience food we enjoy today. Ready-made sandwiches, microwave meals, boil in the bag – they all started back then.

But Findus Crispy Pancakes were more than just a convenience – they had a cult following. To a Persian kid growing up in England, they were a total revelation, miles apart from anything I usually ate at home. The elusive chicken curry flavour was quite a taste sensation, but it is the minced beef version that I still crave today.

Sadly, they were discontinued some time ago and, although they are brought back every now and then, they really don't taste the same as they used to. With the salt, sugar, additives and colourings reduced or removed, they are a sanitised shadow of their former childhood glory.

So a while back, I set about creating my own version and was astonished to find that I had managed to make it really rather similar to the original. Simplicity is key and the ingredients I added have pretty much matched the recipe itself, so now I never need miss them for too long as I can conjure up the same comfort in under an hour.

If that's not a little slice of breadcrumb-coated nostalgia, I don't know what is. I very much hope you love them as much as I do.

MAKES 8

For the pancakes

100g plain flour

2 medium eggs

200ml full fat milk

50ml cold water

50g unsalted butter, melted

a generous pinch of salt

In a large frying pan over a medium heat, drizzle in enough vegetable oil to lightly coat the pan (about 2-3 tablespoons) and begin softening your onions, cooking them until browned around the edges.

Add the minced beef and immediately break it down, almost mashing it into a fine texture. While it is still raw, add all the spices (turmeric, garlic granules, paprika, celery salt and pepper) along with the tomato purée and really work them into the meat as it cooks.

Once the mince is cooked but not browned/crisped up, add the gravy and boiling water. Stir until dissolved and remove the pan from the heat, allowing it to cool.

For the filling

1 large onion, very finely
 chopped
350g minced beef (15-20% fat)
1 tsp paprika (not smoked or
 pimenton)
1 tsp ground turmeric
1 tsp garlic granules
1 tsp celery salt
1 heaped tsp tomato purée
generous mill of black pepper
2 tbsp of beef gravy granules
250ml boiling water
vegetable oil

For the coating

4 medium eggs
150g golden/orange fine
 breadcrumbs

To make your pancake batter, combine all the ingredients together in a mixing bowl, whisking out any lumps in the batter, then pour the mixture into a measuring jug.

Preheat a large frying pan over a medium heat and drizzle about a teaspoon of oil into the centre and slowly pour ⅛ of the mixture on top, making a thin pancake approximately 6in (15cm) in diameter. As soon as bubbles appear on the surface, flip the pancake over without letting either side brown too much (approx. 30-40 seconds if using gas).

Once both sides are done, remove and place on a plate between layers of greaseproof paper and allow to cool. Repeat until all 8 pancakes are done, then set aside.

Place the breadcrumbs in a shallow bowl and beat the eggs in a small bowl, then divide the cooled meat mixture into 8 portions. Place one pancake on a clean surface and top with one portion of the meat mix. Push the mixture to one side of the pancake (so you can fold the other half over it easily) and using a pastry brush, brush the edges with egg and pinch to seal as best you can.

Carefully brush one side of the pancake with beaten egg and coat well in the breadcrumb mixture, then repeat on the other side. Repeat by brushing each side carefully with egg and once again coating each side in breadcrumbs. This will ensure a super crunchy coating and will also enable you to pinch shut any edges that wouldn't seal initially. Repeat until all pancakes are done.

In a large frying pan, add 3cm oil and bring to frying temperature. Once hot (but not smoking), fry the pancakes briefly (a minute or so) until golden and crisp on each side. Remove with a slotted spoon and place onto a plate lined with kitchen paper. Serve immediately. If you prefer to bake them, preheat the oven to 220C/200C Fan/Gas 7, bake for 20 minutes and serve.

Sabrina Ghayour is the host of Sabrina's Kitchen supper club and the author of several cookbooks including **Persiana Everyday** *and* **Bazaar**

Melissa Thompson

BARBECUED PORK RIBS

Our barbecues were always different from other people's. Dad was in the Navy and would bring back food ideas from wherever he had been. He was the first person I knew who used ketchup as an ingredient rather than a stand-alone sauce. He loved feeding people and, whenever the barbecue was lit, it felt like a celebration. I remember the anticipation as the food was cooking, the excitement of having to wait. I've always gravitated towards that.

Where my friends' barbecues had burgers, bangers and chicken that was burnt on the outside and raw in the middle, we had my dad's belly pork ribs. To me, then uninitiated in cooking, they seemed so intriguing and complex. For a start, they needed more cooking than everything else. And they offered so much more texturally and flavour-wise than anything else cooked over coal.

First, there was the caramelised sticky exterior. Then, the slight resistance on first bite before the meat yielded, giving way to layers of fat that, rendered over the coals, almost collapsed into liquid in the mouth. And, of course, the flavour: sweet, tangy, smoky and savoury all at the same time. Those ribs taught me a lot about food – the importance of time, of layering flavour – and as I got into barbecuing, it was these I most wanted to perfect.

When, finally, I cracked it, my family came to mine for a barbecue. My brother took a bite, then turned to Dad and announced that my ribs had taken his top spot. Mum nodded in agreement, while Dad took it graciously, even, perhaps, with a hint of pride.

My secret ingredient is crispy onions, melted into the baste before it's painted onto the ribs. It has a deep sweetness that sings and gives the ribs a brilliant stickiness. They are best on a barbecue, shared with loved ones, but they are also really good in an oven – I've given both methods here.

SERVES 4

8 skinless belly pork ribs, about 3cm thick

For the baste

4 tbsp tomato ketchup

2 tbsp crispy onions

1 tbsp cider vinegar (white wine and rice vinegar also work)

1 tbsp honey

1 tbsp light soy sauce

1 garlic clove, grated

Put all the baste ingredients in a saucepan and cook over a low-medium heat for 8 minutes. If it thickens too much, add a dash of water. Remove from the heat and blend using a stick blender or in a food processor until smooth.

Mix all the rub ingredients together, place the ribs on a tray and sprinkle the rub over them. Ensure they are totally covered, then leave to rest while you prepare the barbecue (for how to cook in an oven, see below).

Light your barbecue for indirect cooking. Pile between 10 and 15 medium-sized charcoal pieces to the side of the bottom grate. Once they're ready – white and glowing – spread them out, but still just on one side of the grate.

For the rub

1 tbsp paprika (ideally sweet, but any will do)

1 tbsp dried oregano

1 tsp garlic powder

1 tsp onion powder (optional)

1 tsp cumin, ground

1 tsp black pepper, ground

1 tsp salt

Place the cooking grate over the coals and sear the ribs directly over the heat for a few minutes each side, until sealed. Then lay them on the opposite side of the grate to the heat. Close the lid and leave for 30 minutes. Aim for the barbecue to be about 140C – if your barbecue doesn't have a temperature gauge, you should be able to comfortably hold your hand 15cm above the coals for about 6-8 seconds. Adjust the temperature using the bottom vents – to increase the temperature, open them more to allow more air in. To reduce the heat, limit the airflow by partially closing the vents.

With a brush, baste the ribs with the sauce. Close the lid again and leave for 30 minutes. Repeat at least three times, always checking the coals are still putting out enough heat. If not, top them up, a couple of extra pieces at a time.

Once the ribs are dark and sticky – the total cooking time will be around 2 hours – remove from the heat and leave to rest for 10 minutes. Serve with a sharp fennel salad.

If cooking in an oven, preheat to 200C/180C Fan/Gas 6 and place ribs in the oven on a tray. Cook for 10 minutes, then reduce heat to 150C/130C Fan/Gas 2 and cook for 30 minutes. Baste all over with the sauce and return to the oven for 30 minutes. Repeat at least three times. Once the ribs are dark and sticky, remove from the oven, rest and serve.

Melissa Thompson is an award-winning food writer who runs the Fowl Mouths food and recipe project. She is a vocal advocate for the promotion of Black and ethnic minority people in food

Melek Erdal

YER DEMIR GÖK BAKIR

When I first arrived in the UK I would see dreams of my grandmother. I learned what it meant to miss someone before I learned the words to utter it. I would retrace the etchings of her face in my mind, try to breathe in her smell and relive the touch of her soft skin.

As I got older and the memories of her were fading like smoke, I became occupied with chasing. I was chasing her face, her voice, her smell... the feelings of home. Cooking is chasing. Chasing her, chasing home, capturing it for a moment, knowing who I am for a moment.

On the telephone, talking to her, I would have to explain why we could not go back to see her. That we were not yet citizens; we could stay but could not leave. That if we went back, we could not return. As I explained, she listened in silence and uttered the words "*yer demir, gök bakir*", "iron earth, copper sky". I would later understand those words to mean the feeling of hopelessness, helplessness, being stuck, as they say, between a rock and a hard place.

And to be away from home is to be in a chase to keep it alive. Still chasing her face, home is the space between an iron earth and a copper sky.

This dish reminds me of grandmother and village cooking. Koftas made from humble bulgur wheat. Homemade yoghurt, the mother of which was kept alive for many years. The copper dish that I serve it in, from our village. Remnants, fragments of home.

SERVES 4

For the bulgur kofta

200g fine bulgur wheat

250ml boiling water

2 tsp salt

1 egg

2 tbsp flour

For the lamb kofta

250g lamb mince

1 small onion

50g breadcrumbs

20g parsley

1 tsp salt

1 tsp black pepper

300g spinach

2 tsp Aleppo chilli flakes

3 tbsp olive oil

First, begin to make your bulgur kofta by soaking the bulgur wheat and salt in a bowl with the boiling water. Cover with a cloth and rest for 15 minutes. This is enough to soften and cook the fine bulgur wheat.

Place the bulgur in a larger mixing bowl, add the flour and egg, and mix and knead thoroughly until it forms a dough. Once the dough has formed, dust a large flat tray with flour and begin rolling small marble-sized koftas with the dough. Once finished, give your tray a shake to cover your koftas in the flour, cover with a cloth and set aside in the fridge.

Next, begin to make your lamb kofta by roughly blitzing your onion, parsley, breadcrumbs, salt and pepper in a blender. Place the lamb in a large mixing bowl and add your blended mix. Knead/mix thoroughly and begin the same process of rolling marble-sized koftas onto a large flat tray. Cover and refrigerate until ready to cook.

For the tomato sauce

2 tomatoes

2 tsp tomato purée

3 tbsp olive oil

pinch of salt

For the garlic yoghurt

150g yoghurt

1 garlic clove

pinch of salt

For the chilli butter

75g salted butter

1 tbsp Aleppo chilli

1 tsp tomato purée

For your tomato sauce, simply grate two large tomatoes into a small saucepan (the skin should naturally separate as you grate, you can discard this). Add your oil, tomato purée, and salt, and heat until it begins to simmer. Simmer for 10 minutes at low heat and set aside.

For your garlic yoghurt, place the yoghurt in a bowl, grate in your garlic, add a pinch of salt and mix.

Cook your bulgur koftas in boiling water for 5 minutes, much as you would pasta, then drain.

In a frying pan, add your 3 tablespoons olive oil and heat until the pan is hot. Add the lamb koftas and cook until browned and caramelised. Keep stirring the koftas with a wooden spoon – this should take around 15 minutes. Then add the drained bulgur koftas to the pan and fry for a further 5 minutes. The bulgur ones will brown and absorb all the flavour from the lamb. If you don't have a large enough pan, feel free to do this in batches. Finally, add your spinach and Aleppo chilli and give it a final toss.

Only make your chilli butter when ready to serve. In a small saucepan melt the butter and then add the purée and Aleppo chilli. Keep on a medium heat until it starts to froth. Keep an eye on it and keep stirring. Once it starts browning and you see sediment forming, take off the heat. This should take around 6-7 minutes.

To serve and assemble, place your kofta mix on a large serving dish. Drizzle over some of the yoghurt, then the tomato sauce, and top with your delicious chilli butter and a final sprinkle of Aleppo chilli flakes. To be shared.

Melek Erdal is a cook and food writer who works with food sustainability charities Felix Project and Made in Hackney and appears on BBC Radio 4's The Kitchen Cabinet

Andi Oliver

HONEY-BAKED CHICKEN WINGS AND SWEETCORN PUDDING

Oh my sweetcorn pudding… A dish of dreams. The first time I encountered it was about 20 years ago at a party in West London. The brilliantly talented American chef Ashbell McElveen was cooking a vast universe of delicious dishes for his then new London restaurant. I was with my darling friend Neneh Cherry and neither of us had ever tasted anything like it. It was instant enchantment. We have since discovered it's an American Southern soul food classic. Sweetcorn pudding and fried chicken, anyone? Yes, yes Lord! Ashbell was kind enough to give us his recipe on the night. It was love at first bite – creamy, soothing and delectable. It went straight into the family repertoiré. We make this every Christmas, birthday, barbeque, summer picnic – any excuse basically and nearly every time, I remember that first time.

SERVES 2-3

For the sweetcorn

340g tinned sweetcorn

3 eggs

300ml double cream

90g unsalted butter, melted

15g caster sugar

3 fat cloves garlic, chopped

good pinch of sea salt

handful of flat leaf parsley

For the chicken wings

1 medium onion, peeled and roughly chopped

4 cloves garlic puréed with 10ml olive oil

1-1.5kg chicken wings

1 lemon, cut in half

1 tbsp garam masala

1 tsp smoked paprika

2 bird's eye chillies, finely chopped

300ml honey

good splash olive oil

To make the sweetcorn, preheat the oven to 180C/160C Fan/ Gas 4, and blitz the cream, eggs, melted butter, sugar and salt in a food processor. Then throw 3 tablespoons of the sweetcorn, as well as the parsley and garlic, into the mix and give it one more blitz so that it's all thoroughly combined. Tip the remaining sweetcorn into a deep oven-proof casserole dish (1.5-2 litre capacity) and pour over the mixture, give it a little stir to combine. Carefully place the casserole into the oven for about 1 hour or until the pudding is set.

Serve with anything you like, including these delicious easy to make chicken wings.

To prepare the wings, put the onion and garlic in a food processor or blender with 10ml olive oil and blitz to a purée. Wash the wings in cold water, drain well and place in a large bowl. Squeeze over the juice of the lemon, then add the spices, onion, garlic purée and chopped chillies and rub in thoroughly, making sure everything is fully coated.

Lay the wings in an even layer in a deep baking tray and place in the oven for 65 minutes, turning halfway through. When the time is up, drizzle the honey all over the chicken wings and return to the oven for 15 minutes until sticky.

Andi Oliver is a chef, broadcaster and singer, and the co-founder of the Wadadli Kitchen and Wadadli Roadside restaurants in East London

Ruby Bhogal

RUBY'S INDIAN CHILLI CHICKEN

My obsession with food started early. I feel blessed to have a rich cultural background, which is the foundation and motivation for much of what I do, cook and eat. This dish is inspired by my first trip to India when I was seven years old. While other kids at school were going to Disneyland on holiday, I was going to Dulowal, the small village in Punjab where my mum grew up.

Everything was so different. These days, I see "different" as a positive thing, but as a naïve, young, impressionable seven-year-old girl, different was, well... different... and at the time, I showed minimal gratitude for this incredible, eye-opening trip. I was sceptical about everything, about everyone and about anything I ate. Now, though, through more mature eyes, I see the value in having experienced the beauty of India at a young age. My love affair with not only the country, but the food, was born.

This is my take on the only dish that seven-year-old Rubes would eat when she first visited India. She found familiarity in the chicken and the garam masala, but also a sense of intrigue in the myriad flavours that made up the dish.

This, for me, brings a warming air of nostalgia and a wave of pride. Food is one journey I will never tire of.

For the chicken and marinade

700g chicken thighs, skinned, deboned and evenly diced

½ white onion

15g fresh ginger

3 cloves garlic

½ tbsp garam masala

½ tsp black pepper

2 tsp chilli powder

2 tbsp dark soy sauce

3 tbsp water

1 tbsp coriander, chopped

5 tbsp cornflour

3 tbsp plain flour

To finish

1 green pepper, cut into chunks

½ white onion, cut into chunks

bunch of spring onions, sliced

2 tbsp garlic and ginger paste (from marinade)

750ml vegetable oil

For the sauce

1 tbsp honey

1 tbsp rice wine vinegar

2 tbsp dark soy sauce

2 tbsp light soy sauce

1 tsp chilli powder

1 tsp nigella seeds

4 green finger chillies, sliced

120ml water

2 tsp cornflour

Start with the marinade. Pop the onion, garlic and ginger into a food processor and blitz to a paste. Set aside 2 tablespoons of the paste before adding the remaining ingredients, apart from the chicken and both kinds of flour. Blitz until combined.

Transfer to a bowl with the chicken and mix. Leave to marinate in the fridge for a few hours/overnight.

Now start pulling the dish together by making the sauce. In a bowl, mix all the ingredients together except the cornflour. Mix 1 tablespoon of the sauce with the cornflour before adding back into the bowl. Leave to one side.

Time to fry the chicken. As much as deep frying is not healthy, it is bloody delicious and what this dish needs. Either use a deep fat fryer or pour 750ml oil into a saucepan and bring to 180C. Just before frying, add the cornflour and plain flour to the chicken and mix.

Fry the chicken in batches for about 2-3 minutes until golden brown before placing on kitchen roll to help soak up any excess oil.

To finish the dish, add a glug of oil to a large frying pan or wok before adding the set-aside onion and garlic paste. Let that cook and brown slightly before adding the green pepper and remaining white onion. Cook for about 2 minutes – we don't want to overcook these and they still need a bit of bite when it comes to serving.

Give the sauce a good stir before adding it to the pan. Allow the sauce to thicken before adding in the chicken, stirring well to ensure everything is coated in that lovely, sticky, rich sauce. Take off the heat, transfer to a dish, and sprinkle the sliced spring onions on top before tucking in. Perfect as a snack on its own or with a side of fried rice, white rice, naan breads, salad, raita... basically anything and everything.

Ruby Bhogal was a finalist on The Great British Bake Off. *She is now a food columnist and regular chef on* Steph's Packed Lunch *on C4 and has launched her own company, Baked by Rubes*

Rachel Roddy

CONIGLIO ALLA CACCIATORA

Looked at on a satellite map, our building looks like a squared figure of eight. If you zoom in close and put a finger on the bottom of the bottom loop, which sits on Piazza Testaccio, the pad of your finger should be more or less pressing on our flat. Now move the finger to the top right-hand corner of the top loop, the location of a trattoria called Il Bucatino.

When I moved to Rome 16 years ago, it was at Il Bucatino that I tasted many classic Roman dishes for the first time: *pasta e ceci* (pasta and chickpea soup), *fagioli con le cotiche* (beans with pork rind), *coda alla vaccinara* (oxtail braised with celery). It is my first time eating *coniglio alla cacciatora* – braised rabbit hunter's-style – that sticks in my mind like a Post-it: how bold I felt ordering rabbit and how normal it was for my Sicilian partner; how the tender meat fell from the bones; the puddle of thickened and brown juices with vinegar finish, the rosemary needle stuck in my tooth and the gesturing hint of the man at the next table urging me to eat with my fingers.

In Italy, rabbit meat, both wild and farmed, is considered quite ordinary and is easy to get hold of. It is often recommended by doctors as a good first meat to introduce to weaning babies (as is horse meat, which is readily available in pasteurised jars, too). My mother-in-law would make a tame version of this dish for my son, when he was very young, mincing the meat finely. He would eat it greedily. Once he learned to talk, he learned to refuse it, but now, at nine, he is sucking on bones again, particularly when I make a version with chicken.

You find variations of this dish all over Italy, some with tomatoes and peppers, others with porcini and locally available herbs and wine. The Roman version is maybe the simplest – the meat browned, seasoned with a fine confetti of chilli and rosemary (whose sturdy, wild scent, all sap green and camphor, is vital here), the whole lot drowned in wine, then simmered until done.

Just the thought of making this dish makes me happy – not just because any dish that calls for a glass of wine for the pan requires one for the cook, but because of the roaring scent rising up from the chopping board, the golden crust on the meat, the mighty whoosh the wine makes as it hits the pan, and the warm scent that fills the kitchen as the dish bubbles away, my specs clouded with steam and my head with extraordinary memories.

You can, if you wish, substitute chicken for the rabbit – whether you are feeding a weaning infant or not.

5 tbsp extra virgin olive oil

1.5kg rabbit (a small one, jointed, or a mixture of legs and thighs)

2 garlic cloves

1 small chilli pepper, or a good pinch of dried chilli

2 sprigs of fresh rosemary

salt and black pepper

300ml white wine, plus extra if needed

1 tbsp red wine vinegar

a handful of pitted black olives

Cut the rabbit into about 12 pieces. In a deep sauté pan, large enough to fit the meat in a single layer, warm the olive oil over a medium heat. Add the meat pieces, skin-side down and cook until the skin forms a golden crust, then turn them over and do the same on the other side. Don't rush – it will take about 15 minutes.

While the meat is browning, chop the garlic, chilli and needles from one rosemary sprig very finely. Once the meat has browned, sprinkle with the chopped garlic, chilli and rosemary, season with salt and pepper, add the whole sprig of rosemary, pour over the white wine, cover the pan and turn the heat down to low.

Cook the meat, turning from time to time, until the thighs feel very tender when prodded with a fork, and the meat is surrounded by thick gravy – 45-75 minutes depending on the rabbit (if you are using chicken, the cooking time will be shorter). If the pan seems a little dry, add a little more wine. In the last minutes of cooking add the vinegar and the olives, stir, and cook for a minute more, before dividing between warm plates.

Rachel Roddy is a food writer and author based in Rome; she has a regular column in The Guardian *and her books include* An A-Z of Pasta *and* My Kitchen in Rome

Helen Goh

CHAR KWAY TEOW

Mum was the real chef in our family. Not only did she cook multiple delectable courses for dinner every night, but each dish would be selected carefully according to the season, how each of us was feeling and the particular energetic properties (yin and yang) of the foods. For the hyperactive Goh clan, Char Kway Teow was deemed "too heaty" or yang. But we loved it so much that Dad defiantly took it upon himself to master the dish. He would cook it every fortnight or so, announcing his intention daringly in front of Mum (who would look on disapprovingly). On the day, he would spend the morning shopping for bouncy fishcake and prawns, pungent garlic chives and fresh rice noodles, then slicing and chopping them meticulously and laying them out on the bench while we drooled with anticipation. It was pure theatre, Dad duelling with the wok hei or breath of the wok – taming it just enough to leave the noodles with the dish's distinctively charred taste. Scooping up the slippery wide ribbons onto a large serving plate, he'd bring out seven pairs of chopsticks. Even Mum could not resist.

2 tbsp lard or vegetable oil

2 cloves garlic, roughly chopped

10 large prawns, peeled

100g Chinese fishcake, thinly sliced

400g fresh rice-flour noodles (kway teow)

½ tsp sugar

½ tsp salt

60ml dark soy sauce

30ml light soy sauce

50ml chicken stock

2 large eggs

¼ tsp ground white pepper

150g beansprouts

40g Chinese chives (also known as flat chives, garlic chives or flowering chives), cut into 5cm lengths

Heat lard or oil in a wok over medium-high heat. When the fat starts to shimmer, add the garlic and fry for about 10 seconds, or until it just begins to take on some colour. Add the prawns and fishcake and cook for 30 seconds, then add the noodles, sugar and ¼ teaspoon of the salt. Toss gently with a spatula until the noodles soften – about 2 minutes.

Add the dark soy, light soy and chicken stock, and continue to stir-fry for a minute more. Make a well in the centre by pushing all the noodles to the edges of the wok, then crack the eggs into the well. Break the yolks lightly with the spatula, then sprinkle with the remaining ¼ teaspoon of salt and the pepper. Fold the noodles over the eggs, covering them entirely, then scatter the bean sprouts and chives on top.

Cook, undisturbed for 15 seconds, then, using a folding action to avoid breaking up the noodles too much, gently stir-fry for a couple of minutes until the sprouts and chives just wilt. A distinct character of this dish is a slightly charred taste, so don't be afraid to crank the heat up so the noodles really get the 'breath' of the wok. Serve onto two plates, with sambal oelek on the side.

Melbourne-born pastry chef Helen Goh is a long-time collaborator of Yotam Ottolenghi; she co-wrote their book, Sweet

Merlin Labron-Johnson

WILD DUCK TOURTE

My parents didn't go to restaurants when I was a child. It wasn't that they didn't like food – they simply didn't have the money. We ate well at home, but it was healthy, balanced, nutritious food rather than anything fancy. I remember lots of rice, salads, pulses and stews. Once a year, however, for a reason that now escapes me, we would go for lunch at a pub called The Duke of York in a small village on Dartmoor. It was one of the rare occasions that our whole family would get together and there would often be 10 or 12 of us around the table.

The pub was a tiny 15th-century inn, with a thatched roof, and served hearty home-cooked meals to a predominantly farming community – an idyllic country pub of a kind that is now virtually extinct. There were two menus, one for adults and one for children and, although the latter generally sounded more appealing, there was one dish on the adult menu that I couldn't resist ordering: "Duck Parcels".

To a nine year old, brought up on brown rice and lentils, nothing in the world seemed more sophisticated than the idea of going out and eating a duck. The fact that it was advertised as coming in a "parcel" only added to the exhilaration. And it was delicious, too, golden puff pastry giving way to a rich duck filling, heavy on the black pepper and moist with ale. I ordered it every year.

Decades later, when I opened my first restaurant in London, I put "pithiviers of wild duck" on my opening menu. It was the dish that helped make the restaurant famous, with critics raving about it. I should have called it "Duck Parcels à la Duke of York". I have been developing the recipe over the years and in winter it continues to make an appearance on my menu at Osip. This is the latest version.

400g puff pastry, rolled to the
  thickness of a £1 coin

1 wild duck

1 partridge breast

40g pork back fat

8 juniper berries, crushed

black pepper

50ml Armagnac or brandy

4 cabbage leaves, blanched and
  well drained of any water

1 egg, beaten

Cut the pastry into 4 circles a little bit larger than the size of a CD. Set aside in the fridge. Remove the breasts and legs from the duck. Remove the skin from the duck breasts and cut in half crossways. Season the breast pieces and stack one half on top of the other so that you have a thicker wedge, almost resembling a square. Wrap this in a cabbage leaf and put in the fridge to chill.

Put the pork fat and partridge meat through the mincer. Take the meat from the duck legs and finely dice, saving the skin for something else. Fold the diced leg meat through the minced partridge and pork fat along with about half of the beaten egg and the booze. Season with salt, lots of pepper and the crushed juniper. Fry a little bit of this mixture to test the seasoning. This is your "farce".

Preheat the oven to 180C/160C Fan/Gas 4.

Remove the wrapped mallard breasts from the fridge. Lay the remaining two cabbage leaves on a bench and add a spoonful of farce to each one. Spread it out in a little circle and sit a mallard breast on top. Now cover the breasts in a thin layer of the farce and bring the edges of the cabbage leaf up around it so that the whole thing is wrapped in a leaf. You should have a mallard breast wrapped in a leaf, wrapped in farce, wrapped in a leaf. Place each of these bundles on a disk of puff pastry and top with another. Pinch and crimp the edges so that they are sealed. Add a drop of milk to the remainder of the beaten egg and use this to brush the top of the pies.

Bake the pies in the oven for about 25 minutes or until they have reached a core temperature of around 57C. Leave to rest for 4-5 minutes before carving. Serve with a game sauce, some preserved fruit and a bitter leaf salad.

Merlin Labron-Johnson is chef-founder of Michelin-starred restaurant Osip and The Old Pharmacy wine bar and épicerie in Bruton, Somerset

Rosie Mackean

SPAGHETTI ALLE VONGOLE

I first discovered clams on a trip to Portugal when I was eight years old. My dad had ordered me a bowlful with bread and chips, and I drank every last sip of the winey, briny liquor they had made.

That was it: I was hooked on shellfish. From then on, I would order it every time we went out, even though I often had to make do with moules marinière, as clams were hard to come by in Somerset. Still, as long as I had something starchy to soak up that sauce, I was happy. I always felt so grown up when my plate of clams or mussels arrived with all the extra crockery it required. It made me feel like a VIP, while my brothers tucked into sausages, chips and beans from the kids' menu. There aren't many sounds that truly inspire hunger, but for me the clinking of shells in a pan is one of them – along with ice tinkling in a glass. It is so unique, so evocative.

When I first had spaghetti alle vongole, I realised pasta was the best carb for soaking up that addictive clam juice. It did half the work for you. No more messy fingers: just slippery, succulent strands and sweet clam nuggets. As I started to spend more and more time in Italy, pasta alle vongole in its various forms became an essential dish for me to try wherever I was – a port in Liguria, canal side in Venice or under twinkling lights in Rome. I cannot look past it on a menu. It is a dish that has become utterly transportive. When I make it for myself at home, it takes me away. Back to hot summer nights in Italy. Back to a dark booth in a Somerset pub with my family, happily bickering with my brothers. Back to Portugal, sitting on my dad's knee, my bowl to my lips. To me, clams mean love.

SERVES 2

500g fresh clams (verace/ telline)

40ml olive oil

3 cloves of perfectly ripe garlic, sliced - no green centres or shooting tops, please. The best have a rusty pink hue to the skin, which is tight, shiny and firm around the clove.

150ml dry white wine – something you would drink

2 salted anchovies

2-3 dried red peperoncini,

Start by soaking your clams in cold, salted water for about an hour to purge any sand. Then drain them off and discard any that are open or broken. Give the shells a good rinse and a scrub if particularly dirty.

Bring a large pot of water to the boil and season as you would a soup - taste it to check you are happy.

Heat the oil in your pan - a wide saucepan or sauté pan with a lid is the best for helping the clams steam. Hold your hand above the oil to check the temperature, as if you were about to give it a high five. When it is toasty warm, it's ready for garlic.

It is important to be completely set now for the rest of the cooking - everything you need should be prepped and ready to go as timing is important. Drop your spaghetti into your boiling water and stir well to separate. Immediately after, add

crushed, or ½ tsp dried red
chilli flakes

a large handful of fresh flat-leaf
parsley, finely chopped

30g cold unsalted butter, diced

salt and pepper

250g best-quality dried
spaghetti

your sliced garlic, chilli and anchovies to the oil. They should sizzle for less than 30 seconds before you add your clams. Quickly toss in the white wine for a briny facial before clamping a tight lid on. I like to shake the pan with the lid on a little so I know my clams are well distributed.

After about 3 minutes, check your clams. If they are 90% opened, leave the lid on for 30 more seconds to make sure they are on their way, after which discard any that are unopened. Then using tongs, lift your spaghetti from the water and add into the clam pan. Take a couple of ladlefuls of pasta water and top up the liquid to just a centimetre under the surface of the spaghetti. This method is called pasta risottata – essentially you cook your spaghetti as you would a risotto, resulting in a thick, starchy sauce and pasta that has absorbed all that ambrosial clam juice. Keep the spaghetti and clams simmering merrily, moving every so often, until the spaghetti is cooked and the sauce has reduced in the pan by about half. If at any point you are worried it is getting too dry, then add a splash more pasta liquid.

When you are happy with how the spaghetti is cooked, remove from the heat and add the cold diced butter and chopped parsley. Toss or stir really well for a minute or so – this final agitation with the fat and the starch and the sauce are what brings it all together. Add an additional drizzle of your best olive oil, if you like, before serving in bowls with plenty of bread ready for dipping in any leftover juices and large glasses of white wine.

Rosie Mackean is a former chef at Café Murano and now teaches masterclasses in pasta-making and cooks private dinners for clients

Rose Prince

CHEESE FONDUE

My grandmother insisted that the French region known as the Riviera was truly the Alpes Maritimes, the coastal Alps – where a beach and a ski resort had less than an hour's drive between them. An Anglo-American, she lived in the Swiss Alps in the post-war years recovering from TB then decided, as a divorcee, that life in the South of France would be better than that in stuffy England. Her home for the next 50 years, a farmhouse minutes away from the Mediterranean near Antibes, would in so many ways shape my own future. A baby on my first visit, I was 30 on my last.

My grandmother Mary did not just love eating – the next meal was on her mind as soon as she finished the last. When we stayed with her, the family would plan lunch and dinner at a morning conference. She would shop for the ingredients, though she would not cook – she and her second husband Vadim, our beloved "Grandva", ran a business – and the resulting meals, made by her cook Jacqueline, were epic in their length and heavenly conviviality.

All of us who stayed at La Ferme Blanche remember those decades with gratitude. Siblings and cousins still talk about Jacqueline's dishes. Most were local, as the region has very particular ingredients: sardines, moules, beautiful salad leaves from the coast, *nouilles* – the buttery noodles of the Nicoise area – raviolis filled with meat, also served buttered with grated mountain cheeses. She made a superb salad Niçoise, peeling the tomatoes so they could drink up the vinaigrette.

We ate giant artichokes, also with her fiery vinaigrette, tomatoes and round, pale green courgettes stuffed with rice and herbs, and we all loved a supper of lean local sausages eaten with oozy, yellowish pomme purée. We rarely ate prime cuts or expensive meats, but veal, from the foothills of the Alps, was inexpensive and regularly on the table in many forms – a meat that my grandmother had learned to love when living in the mountains.

Cheeses from the same region were served daily, always with a green salad – never biscuits. Very occasionally, when it rained in summer and we ate indoors, Jacqueline made a pot of cheese fondue. I think she rather disapproved of the dish, worrying about my grandmother's cholesterol levels – but for us it was a great if somewhat hard-to-digest treat. I never knew her recipe, but this is the one I like to use. I heartily approve of adding the "cheese triangle". It does wonders for the texture.

2 tsp cornflour

40ml kirsch

400g Gruyère cheese, grated

400g Emmenthal cheese, grated

1 foil-wrapped cream cheese triangle (Vache Qui Rit or similar)

250ml Sauvignon Blanc wine

1-2 sourdough baguettes, cut into bite-sized chunks

You will need either a fondue set with burner, or something that will keep the fondue hot and runny while it is on the table. The pan, or fondue pot, must have a heavy base – a cast iron casserole dish is ideal.

Whisk together the cornflour and kirsch in a small bowl and set aside. Put all the cheeses and wine into the fondue pot and set over a low heat. Stir continually as the cheese melts into the wine then begins to bubble. The process takes about 15-20 minutes – the alcohol will be "cooked out". When the cheese has melted, quickly stir in the cornflour and kirsch mixture and bubble for a minute more.

Transfer the pot to the table, placed over a burner or other heater. Spear the bread chunks onto forks and dip away. Finish the meal with a green salad or fruit.

Rose Prince is a food writer, the former in-house chef at Books for Cooks in London's Notting Hill and the author of several books including The New English Kitchen *and* Dinner & Party

Cyrus Todiwala

MORI DAAR

Food is all about memories, and that's a critical part of why I cook. I was badly asthmatic as a child and my Masi, my mother's sister, would spend hours with me as I heaved and sighed and coughed. When I was better, she'd make scrambled eggs – delicious, buttery, creamy, soft and runny scrambled eggs made on an old kerosene stove. That's still my all-time favourite, on-the-road comfort food, even at 10 o'clock at night.

The recipe I've chosen here, however, is from the traditional Sunday lunch we had every week: a Parsee classic called *mori daar*, puréed lentils with garlic, cumin and green chilli, which we had accompanied with fried papads and masala-fried fish and plenty of caramelised onion in ghee. At my home in Mumbai I still have the Pyrex bowl – a wedding present to my parents in 1950 – in which my mother served the daal. I still remember the aroma of fish frying in the skillet as she prepared lunch.

Our younger son once told me years ago that "You may be the best cook in the world, but Bapaiji's (paternal grandmother's) daal is the best." I guess my mother's daal was the best, as it is for most Indian men. Given the choice, this would be my last supper. It's simple and comforting, forever etched in my mind – maybe it helps keep the memories of family dining alive. Afterwards, we sit down and slouch and doze off, just like my parents did all those years ago.

SERVES 4

250g toor daal (pigeon pea lentil or har-har daal)

1 tsp turmeric

pinch salt

knob of butter

2 tbsp sunflower or rapeseed oil

1-2 green finger chillies

1 tsp cumin seeds

2-3 cloves garlic

1 tbsp chopped fresh coriander

Preferably buy the toor daal with oil or any oiled daal – this preserves the daal and keeps it fresh, though it needs a good wash. So wash well first with hot water and then with tepid water until the water runs clean. What I do is add the hot water then rub well between the palms of my hands so that it saves on water. Soak well in water about an inch above the surface of the lentils for a few hours, ideally overnight.

When soaked and well absorbed, place in a pot and bring to a boil on a medium heat. When the daal starts to heat up, the water will froth and foam. This has to be skimmed gently and removed. Once this is done add salt and turmeric and stir well. If it still froths, clear the foam and then add the blob of butter. When the lentils are thoroughly cooked purée them with a stick blender or pass through a sieve and beat until they resemble a soup.

Heat the oil in a frying pan and when hot, but not too hot, add the green chillies. As soon as they change colour, add the cumin and garlic and sauté until the garlic is pale golden in colour.

At this stage turn off the heat and keep stirring the pan until the garlic turns a nice light golden brown colour but does not burn. Add this to the daal and scrape the pan clean into the daal, mix well and taste. Season if need be and add the chopped coriander.

Enjoy with some cumin-flavoured rice, some fried fish and a good chutney. A Parsee would add another large blob of butter before serving but that choice is yours.

Cyrus Todiwala MBE owns and runs the Café Spice Namasté group of restaurants in the UK

Tom Parker Bowles

NEAPOLITAN RAGU

The Hotel Excelsior, Ischia, sometime in the early 1980s. Five small children, pink-skinned and salt-stained, sit in the vast dining room, empty save for battalions of black-jacketed waiters. They scurry round us like frantic ants, preparing for the evening's service, polishing glasses, laying tables, gossiping, joshing and stopping occasionally to ruffle our hair. "*Tutto bene?*" they sing, as they bring icy bottles of Coke and endless packs of grissini. Next comes the return chorus, "*Si, tutto bene.*" We're on our annual family holiday to this divine island, just off Naples, and everything is very good indeed.

Our parents and grandparents are upstairs, bathing, as my grandmother calls it, getting dressed for dinner, and preparing for the first Americano of the night. Meanwhile, we are alone, blissfully happy, gathered around our usual table with the crispest and thickest of white tablecloths. Reliving yet another day spent swimming in the sea, eating doughnuts bought from the man on the beach, collecting sea urchins (which we keep in the bidets in our rooms until they die and smell like poo), eating parmigiano or *vongole* or *cozze* for lunch.

But dinner? Dinner is sacred, always the same. We don't even need to ask. Five waiters appear, as they do every night, carrying silver platters covered with silver cloches. They stop, move behind, and place them on the table. Then, with a flourish, they whip off the lids to reveal that great southern Italian classic... spaghetti Bolognese. Of course, we couldn't care less about authenticity. Our only concern was that it was covered with a blizzard of Parmesan. There was chocolate ice cream for pudding. And we had five more days of holiday to go.

SERVES 6-8

- 1–2 tbsp extra virgin olive oil
- 250g rindless pork belly, cut into large chunks
- 250g stewing veal
- 250g beef shin, cut into chunks
- 2 onions, finely chopped
- ½ bottle (375ml) of punchy red wine
- 3 x 400g cans chopped tomatoes
- big pinch of sea salt
- big pinch of dried chilli flakes
- handful of fresh parsley, finely chopped

Heat 1 tablespoon of oil in a large heavy pot over a medium heat and brown the meat, in batches, until well browned – around 5 minutes per batch. Start with the pork as it will release some fat, but add more oil if it starts to stick.

After removing the final batch of meat, tip the onions into the pan and cook over a low heat for about 10 minutes, until soft, stirring and scraping up the crisped bits of meat stuck on the bottom of the pan.

Return all the meat to the pan, add the wine and reduce over a high heat. Add the tomatoes, salt and chilli and simmer very gently for 3-4 hours. Stir every 15 minutes or so, skimming off any excess fat. You may need to add a little water, 100ml at a time, if the sauce begins to stick during the last couple of hours. Scatter on the parsley and serve with cooked spaghetti or fusilli.

Tom Parker Bowles is a food writer, author and restaurant critic for The Mail on Sunday

Thomasina Miers

OUR DEFINITIVE FRIDAY NIGHT FISH PIE

The seemingly endless car journeys of my childhood, gazing out of the window at the grey tarmac of motorways, or Welsh hillsides dotted with the occasional turreted castle, bickering with my siblings... If these are still strong in my memory, so, too, are the arrivals at our respective grandparents' houses. Exclamations of joy, comments on appearances, large whiskies poured and the much-loved dishes we always had on those Friday nights, appearing magically from the depths of the Aga and filling the kitchen with the most delicious smells.

At one grandmother's, it was her leek quiche with buttery shortcrust pastry, plumped up with the molten leeks and golden cheese crust; at the other's, sometimes a bobotie, a dish from her South African childhood, but more often than not her fish pie. In those days, the glimpse of a pink prawn was wonderfully exotic, although the dish itself, I fear, did not always live up to the memory of it, steeped as it was in the pleasure of arrival at that cosy home of tiddlywinks, After Eights and the great outdoors.

Fast forward 40 years and my parents have taken those familiar recipes, including the marmalades, hot hams and waffles, and imprinted on them their own particular mark. They adore cooking – it is a passion that accelerated when we flew the nest, leaving them the time to experiment.

It was about this time that my mother threw down the gauntlet and announced she would no longer cook on Saturday nights. My father met the challenge with his customary mix of feigned amusement and quiet determination. His first Saturday was a day and a half spent in the kitchen grappling with three or four Madhur Jaffrey recipes and the ensuing feast was resplendent, even if it left the kitchen in chaos. His love affair with Heston soon followed and it is from that love that this exquisite fish-pie recipe was developed, using my grandmother's inherited version, my mother's inherent skill for making simple ingredients sing and my father's meticulous interpretation of Heston's perfect mash. My mother does the base of the pie and my father the top, a sinfully delicious mass of silky smooth, mustard-and-Cheddar rich potatoes.

The result is a jaw-droppingly mouth-watering, deeply pleasing plate of food that restores far more than basic hunger. It is a dish we unconsciously pray for as we walk through the door, now with a small brood of our own, arms reached out for warm hugs and that tumbler of whisky and soda thrust towards us.

SERVES 8

2 medium onions, finely sliced

fine sea salt and freshly ground
   black pepper

½ tsp brown sugar

extra virgin olive oil

1kg mixed white fish, skinned

200g smoked, undyed haddock,
   skinned

400ml full fat milk

about 50 peeled prawns,
   preferably MSC

3 hard-boiled eggs

For the white sauce

100g butter

4 heaped tbsp plain or spelt
   flour

400ml fish stock

anchovy essence, to taste

nutmeg, to taste

For the topping

1 kg peeled floury potatoes

200g very cold butter

200ml full fat milk

3 free-range egg yolks

100g Cheddar, Lincolnshire
   Poacher or Comté

1 tbsp wholegrain mustard

1 tbsp Worcestershire sauce

2 tsp good quality horseradish
   sauce

Put a splash of olive oil in a pan, add the onions, sugar and a little salt, and fry gently until caramelised – about half an hour. Cut the fish into even, bite-size pieces.

Bring the milk to the boil, take off the heat, add the fish and leave to cool. Use that milk to make the white sauce, in the usual manner, melting the butter in a pan until sizzling hot, stirring in the flour for a few minutes to cook out its raw taste, then vigorously beating in the milk and stock, little by little, to create a smooth white sauce. Season generously with salt, pepper, nutmeg and the anchovy essence.

Spread the fish in a single layer over the base of a baking dish. Sprinkle evenly with the prawns, followed by the sliced eggs and lastly the onions. Spread the sauce over the top.

To make the mash, cut the potatoes evenly into ½in slices and rinse in cold water. Heat plenty of water to 80C, add the spuds and cook at a constant temperature of 70C for 30 minutes. Drain and rinse under running water to cool. Put the spuds back into the saucepan with cold salted water, bring to a boil and simmer until completely tender. Drain, return to the pan and dry over a low heat.

Cube the butter into a bowl and press the spuds through a potato ricer onto the butter. Fold spud and butter together, then push through a fine sieve. If eating immediately, heat the milk to a simmer and fold into the spuds (otherwise mix in the milk cold and keep somewhere cool). Mix in the rest of the ingredients and don't forget to season.

Spread the potato mix evenly over the white sauce. Bake the dish at 180C/160C Fan/Gas 4 (or in the bottom of the top Aga oven) for 30-40 minutes until puffed up and golden.

Thomasina Miers is a chef and founder of the restaurant chain Wahaca, whose books include Meat-Free Mexican

Rosie Birkett

MY DAD'S SEAFOOD "SIZZLE"

My dad, who we lost when I was 21, was a huge lover of food and drink. He and his two sisters had been brought up by a single mother during rationing and he had a seemingly insatiable appetite that followed him into adulthood. When I was little, this dictated the culinary trajectory of most of our evenings, weekends and family camping holidays in France and Spain.

With my mum beside him navigating, he'd drive us through little villages or along the coast, sniffing out the best spots to eat local fare and always favouring low-key, paper-tablecloth-clad, family-run restaurants, where the food was honest and he could pour the wine – lots of it. If fresh seafood was on the menu, my parents would order it, and I loved to watch as they picked their way through seafood platters, passing me and my sister prawns to peel between our mouthfuls of frites, steak haché and buttered baguette, and telling us stories of their careers as journalists in the 1970s.

Dad's childlike enthusiasm for delicious things infected me from a young age, and it is this – along with my mum's own passion for good food and incredible home cooking – that led to my eventual career as a food writer. He'll never know it – he died a couple of weeks before my university graduation – but I often think about him when I'm cooking and eating, and never more so than when I make this dish.

Dad had certain "signature dishes" and this "seafood sizzle" was one of his favourites. It's a flavourful medley of prawns, squid and bacon, cooked in shedloads of olive oil with spring onions, garlic and chilli, which I think was probably loosely based on *gambas pil pil*, but which he bastardised with smoked bacon. For me, it conjures up memories of my dad cooking happily in the kitchen by the sea in Kent not long before he died, but also of those earlier times in French and Spanish restaurants, peeling prawns and wiping fingers on little lemon-scented wet wipes.

His recipe went through several iterations, sometimes featuring a bit of grated ginger or clams. He would prep for what seemed like hours, meticulously cutting the spring onions, chilli and garlic before frying it all together in a matter of moments. It's best eaten with big hunks of good, crusty bread to soak up the shellfish-heady, bacon-fat infused, garlicky olive oil the seafood should be swimming in.

SERVES 2-4

300g fresh squid, cleaned (ask your fishmonger to do this for you)

1 tbsp lemon juice

a splash of Worcestershire sauce

5 garlic cloves, two crushed, three thickly sliced

4 rashers of smoked, streaky bacon, cut in half and rolled up into tight rolls, fastened with a cocktail stick

100ml extra virgin olive oil

2 large spring onions, cut into matchsticks

½ tsp dried red chilli flakes

1 red chilli, finely sliced

12 shell-on prawns, half peeled and deveined with heads removed, the rest left whole

a handful of flat-leaf parsley, washed and chopped

baguette or crusty bread, to serve

lemon wedges, to serve

Marinate the squid for about an hour before you start cooking. Open up the cone-shaped body section of the squid by cutting down one side with a knife, then score the underside in a crosshatch pattern and cut it into rectangles (about 5cm x 3cm). Cut the tentacle section of each squid in half. Put it in a bowl and add the crushed garlic, a pinch of salt, a grind of pepper (I love white pepper here), the lemon juice, Worcestershire sauce and a slosh of olive oil to coat. Toss it all together in the marinade and refrigerate while you prep the other ingredients.

Half an hour before you cook, take your seafood out of the fridge to bring it up to room temperature. Grab a large, non-stick frying pan or skillet and heat 2 tablespoons of the oil over a medium heat. Add in the bacon and fry, turning, until browning and smelling delicious – a few minutes. Now pour in the rest of the oil, add the sliced garlic, spring onion, dried and fresh chilli, and cook, stirring, for a couple of minutes until the garlic is sizzling.

At this point, add in all your prawns and cook for 2 minutes, shaking the pan to avoid anything catching. After 2 minutes, give everything a good move around, turn the prawns over, add in the squid and its marinade and shake the pan again, making sure the squid is in contact with the pan. Cook for a further 3 minutes or so, until the squid and prawns are just about cooked through, then remove from the heat – they will continue to cook on in the hot oil. Scatter with the parsley and put the pan on a mat in the middle of the table. Ladle into warm bowls, with chunks of bread for dipping, and extra lemon wedges.

Rosie Birkett is a food writer and cookbook author. She writes regularly for BBC Good Food, The Sunday Times *and* Olive; *her books include* A Lot on Her Plate

Xanthe Clay

CHICKEN STOCK

There was always an earthenware pot of chicken stock in the fridge. It lived on the top shelf, underneath the ice compartment of the 1970s Frigidaire in our Islington kitchen. A crisp layer of ivory fat covered the top – no namby-pamby clingfilm in those days – shattered where my mother's ladle had scooped out a crater in the glistening beige gel beneath.

On the stove a white enamel pan might have the makings of the next batch: chicken bones, an onion stuck with a clove, a bay leaf, a phut – pause – phut noise of barely simmering liquid.

I hardly noticed the pervasive, earthy scent. Now my grown-up offspring tell me that the same smell is the smell of home for them, even if I'm more likely to be making my stock prosaically in an electric slow cooker, so there is no soundtrack. My freezer has an entire shelf dedicated to cubes of frozen stock, mostly chicken. I have been known to ask for a doggy bag in a restaurant, just to carry home bones so I can make more stock.

What was the root of this preoccupation with chicken stock? Was it from my mother's culinary inspiration, the Three Graces of post-war British cooking: Elizabeth David, Jane Grigson and Patience Gray? Theirs were the dishes that we ate day to day, beef with olives and noodles, sweetbreads with mushrooms, ox heart braised with orange, in tiny portions as money was tight and Ma was fearful of raising fat daughters. But in fact, chicken stock appears hardly at all in Mrs David's recipes; Gray is similar, and even Grigson has no directions for making it. Chicken stock in every soup, stew and sauce, enriching and bolstering the savoury notes, appears to be a modern culinary tic. It seems my mother was just an early adopter.

the carcass of a roast chicken (the older the chicken, the more gelatine your stock will contain, which will add lip-smacking body to dishes)

1 onion, stuck with a clove (it's fine to use a collection of the tough outer layers of onions, keeping the innards for other recipes)

1 bay leaf

1 small carrot

1 stick of celery (I save sad and floppy stalks and put them in the freezer, ready for the stockpot)

Put the ingredients in a large pan and cover with cold water. Bring to a gentle simmer – just the occasional phut-phut of bubbles breaking the surface. Cook for 2 hours. If you are using a slow cooker, then it will be 4 hours. You can even leave it overnight in the slow cooker, which will make a more intense stock that's good for rustic dishes.

Strain and leave to cool, then chill. Lift off any fat that sets on the surface: this is schmaltz, and you can use it for frying potatoes.

Xanthe Clay is a food writer, cookery author and columnist for The Telegraph

Neil Borthwick

RABBIT À LA JULIETTE

My mum was a French teacher and every summer we would spend nearly two months at a little house my parents had bought in the Vendée. My dad would come out for two or three weeks and spend the whole time doing the place up. He went home more exhausted than when he got there.

The Vendée is a very rural bit of France. It was half an hour to the nearest shops and the local baker would drive his van out around the villages just once a week. I can't remember ever going to restaurants. When we ate out, it was at other people's houses. The locals liked us because we embraced their hospitality and made an effort to speak their language. I wasn't the most academic pupil, but I loved speaking French.

Our closest neighbours were Juliette and Yan-Yan, a salt-of-the-earth couple who had the farm next door. Yan-Yan was well known for his generosity. He had a big barn – *la grange de Yan-Yan* – which was quite a thing. The farm as a whole was pretty unkempt, but the barn was beautiful inside, with a big trestle table for everyone to sit around and a large area for playing *boules vendéennes* – like regular boules, but played with large wooden balls.

Juliette and Yan-Yan were cattle farmers, but they also kept rabbits in hutches in their garden. One morning my mum was chatting with Juliette when, suddenly, she lifted one of the rabbits from its cage, pulled out a knife and dispatched it in front of her. "*On va manger ça demain,*" she said – we'll eat that tomorrow.

Next day, we were invited to Yan-Yan's barn to eat the lapin. The rabbit had been simply stewed with onion, garlic and wine, with mogette beans – a local speciality – on the side. Like all food in the Vendée, it was rustic and no-nonsense, but it was also delicious, washed down with plenty of vin de table and Yan-Yan's homemade blackthorn-leaf liqueur, trousse-pinette, which was amazingly perfumed and incredibly strong. I was only 14 or 15, but this being France, nobody minded me having "*un petit verre*".

Ten years later, when I went to work in south-west France as a young chef, those Vendée holidays stood me in good stead; the French are much more accepting of a Scot who can speak French and cook. But the memory of the happy times in Yan-Yan's barn also gave me a taste for conviviality – everybody eating, drinking, chatting, playing boules. It showed me that hospitality is about giving people a time to remember, the enjoyment of a shared moment. And that, ultimately, is why I do what I do.

1 farmed rabbit, jointed

plain flour, for dusting

olive oil

200g smoked bacon, cut into
    lardons

6 Roscoff onions, peeled and
    chopped

3 heads garlic

4 sprigs thyme

2 bay leaves

3 sprigs rosemary

1kg plum vine tomatoes,
    chopped

1 bottle white wine

Season the rabbit pieces liberally with salt and lightly flour. Sear in olive oil until golden brown and set aside.

Cook the lardons until golden, then add the onions and garlic and continue to cook for 10-15 minutes until nicely softened.

Add the herbs and tomatoes to the pan and cook over a high heat for 10 minutes.

Add the wine to the pan and bring to a simmer.

Add the rabbit to the pan and cook for 45-60 minutes until the leg is cooked.

Remove the garlic and allow to cool before squeezing the pulp from each clove back into the stew. Mix well and check the seasoning.

Sprinkle with chopped parsley and serve at the table, ideally with some mogette beans and a nice glass of something red.

Neil Borthwick is chef and proprietor of the French House restaurant in London's Soho

Lucas Hollweg

GOULASH

The images spool through my mind like an old cine film. Happy faces around a table in the sun. It is the mid 1970s. My mum is glamorous in her flared salopettes and owl-like sunglasses; my sister, dark and pretty; and me, a mousey child with a pageboy haircut and ski-school badges tacked to the sleeve of a too-big jacket. The others in the picture – my dad, grandmother and grandfather – are now sadly no longer around, their smiles preserved only in the flickering celluloid reel of memory.

We are sitting on the terrace at Herr Pfefferkorn's, looking out across pine trees to the snow-topped peaks beyond. It is the cusp of springtime, the mountain air mingled with the smell of chips and Piz Buin. People drink perfumed white wine and foaming glasses of Spaten beer. On the table in front of me is a bowl of *Gulaschsuppe* – goulash soup – the caraway-scented juices stained scarlet with paprika, the meat so soft that it falls into shreds beneath my spoon.

That I have these memories is thanks to my German grandfather, Mops. He was an avid winter sportsman, who had learnt to ski during his schooldays in Switzerland and, as a young man, played ice hockey in the Winter Olympics. In the 1960s, he built a holiday house in the Austrian Alps and, as children, we would come every couple of years for a fortnight in the snow. The chalet smelt of ski wax and pine resin, with a tiled stove in the sitting room and a checked tablecloth on the kitchen table.

Our days were spent skiing and eating. After breakfast, we would set off for the slopes, Mops with an Olympic badge pinned to the band of his felt hat and a bar of Toblerone in the pocket of his padded jacket. Most days, we would buy plates of chips at a mountain cafeteria and sit eating them with a picnic lunch of crusty white Brötchen, filled with soft pork pâté, and a triangle of chocolate for pudding. Lunch at Herr Pfefferkorn's – a cosy restaurant near the top of a chair lift – was a more occasional treat. We would plant our skis and poles in the drifts by the door and waddle out to the terrace in our stiff boots.

The menu was simple and unchanging, a medley of schnitzels, cevapcici – cigar-like meat rissoles – pork steaks with dark mustard, salads with herb-flecked dressings, ice cream with chocolate sauce and Austrian puddings whose names – *Kaiserschmarrn, Germknödel* – seemed borrowed from a fairytale. But it was the goulash soup that always drew me in. In my imagination, it conjured images of smoky middle-European cabins in the woods. It was a soup to cradle the soul.

Fifty years later, I still find myself craving its deep-pile comfort. My version is more stew than soup – and, in truth, peppers, horseradish and pickles never featured back then. But it shares its heart with those childhood bowlfuls, a link, somehow, to those much-missed members of my family and the Germanic part of me – to an innocent time of gingerbread and hut socks, tasselled hats and snowplough turns.

SERVES 4

4 red peppers (or 6-8 long romero peppers)

900g boneless shin of beef, trimmed of external fat and cut into rough 3cm cubes

salt and pepper

2 tbsp olive oil

150g rindless dry-cured smoked streaky bacon (preferably from a whole slab), cut into lardons

3 medium onions, peeled and sliced

4 cloves of garlic, finely chopped

2 whole cloves

2-3 bay leaves

leaves from 4 bushy sprigs of thyme

6 juniper berries, flattened

1 heaped tbsp tomato purée

1 heaped tbsp sweet paprika (not smoked), plus extra for sprinkling

a decent pinch cayenne pepper

2 tsp caraway seeds

200ml red wine

150ml good beef stock

1½ tbsp red wine vinegar

dill pickled cucumbers, sliced, to serve

dill fronds, to serve

For the horseradish cream

250ml thick crème fraîche

¼ of a horseradish root (or more to taste) peeled

1-2 tsp red wine vinegar

salt and pepper

caster sugar

Start with the horseradish cream. Grate the horseradish into a bowl and stir in 1 teaspoon of vinegar. Fold through the crème fraîche until combined, then season well with salt, pepper and a pinch of sugar. Add more vinegar and horseradish to taste. Put in the fridge until needed.

Heat the grill on its highest setting. Put the peppers in a roasting tin, place under the grill and cook, turning often, until blistered on all sides. Place in a bowl and cover tightly with foil or clingfilm. Leave to steam for 20 minutes, then peel off the skins and remove the seeds. Slice or tear the flesh into strips about 1cm wide and place in a bowl.

Preheat the oven to 150C/130C Fan/Gas 2.

On the hob, heat the oil in a cast-iron casserole dish (big enough to hold all the ingredients). Season the beef generously with salt and pepper and cook in batches over a medium heat until lightly browned. Scoop out and add to the peppers, leaving the oil in the pan.

Throw in the lardons and cook over a medium heat for 3-4 minutes until they start to brown, then mix in the onions and a pinch of salt and cook for about 10 minutes until soft and sweet. Stir in the garlic, thyme, cloves, juniper and bay and cook for 5 minutes more.

Mix in the tomato purée, paprika, cayenne and caraway, stir over the heat for 2-3 minutes, then add the beef and peppers. Tip in the red wine, vinegar and stock – the meat should be just covered when pushed into the liquid. Season well and cover the surface with a circle of greaseproof paper. Bring to a simmer, cover with a lid and place in the oven. Leave to cook for 2 ½-3 hours, or until the meat is on the verge of collapse. Taste and season – don't be shy with the salt. Add a little more vinegar if you feel it needs it. Leave to cool and put in the fridge overnight – it will be better for it.

Next day, bring it back to a simmer on the hob and bubble gently until warmed through. Ladle into deep bowls and top with a blob of the horseradish cream, some sliced dill pickles, a sprinkling of dill leaves and a light dusting of extra paprika. Serve with good bread for dunking and mopping.

Lucas Hollweg is a food writer, cook and feast maker, and author of Good Things to Eat

Asma Khan

NARANGI KORMA

My paternal great-grandfather, Lieutenant Colonel Sir Muhammad Ahmed Said Khan, Nawab of Chhatari, played an active role in the transition of India from colonial rule to independence. Under British India, he was the only Indian to hold the post of Governor of United Provinces of Agra and Oudh, later becoming the first Chief Minister of United Provinces and then Prime Minister to the last Nizam of Hyderabad from 1941-46 and again in 1947.

Organising banquets for visiting dignitaries and royalty was an important part of his life. India in the 1930s and 40s went through enormous political change, the dark shadow of Partition loomed on the horizon. Many discussions took place in our home between Indian and British political parties. My great-grandfather travelled to England in 1930 and 1931 to attend the Round Table Conferences on Indian constitutional reform, organised by the British government. On his return, a new ingredient was added to a dish, specially prepared for royal banquets. Oranges joined cashew nuts in this yoghurt-based chicken korma and then were grown in our fruit orchards, surrounding the fortress of Chhatari.

This recipe was given to me by Muhammad Babu, son of the head cook of our family kitchen during my great-grandfather's lifetime. I remember clearly eating this orange korma at a banquet to celebrate my great-grandfather's 90th birthday.

SERVES 6

3 large oranges

8 tbsp melted ghee

150g lotus seeds (makhana)

200g onions, thinly sliced

1 tbsp garlic paste

1 tbsp fresh ginger paste

1 tsp salt

2 tbsp ground coriander

1 tsp chilli powder

50g cashew nuts

50g almonds

180g natural (plain) yoghurt

250ml water

1 tsp ground garam masala

½ tsp ground turmeric

1kg skinless, bone-in chicken thighs

1 large bay leaf

¼ tsp sugar

Wash the oranges thoroughly. Cut one orange in half, from top to bottom, then cut one half into segments with the peel still on. Cover and set aside. Peel the remaining oranges and cut the rind into thin slivers. Squeeze the juice from the oranges and set aside.

In a small pan, heat 1 tbsp of the ghee and fry the lotus seeds. Set aside a small handful of the fried seeds for the garnish. Mix the remaining seeds with a splash of water and grind to a paste.

In a pan, heat the remaining ghee and fry the onions until they are brown and caramelised. Remove with a slotted spoon to a plate to drain. Using a food processor, blitz the onions to a paste. Set aside the remaining ghee in the pan to use later to cook the chicken.

In a food processor, whizz the nuts to a powder. Add this to the yoghurt and then thin the mixture down with a little water.

While the onion paste is frying, mix the lotus seed, garlic and ginger pastes into the yoghurt and ground-nut mixture, along with the salt, coriander and chilli powder. Then stir in the browned onion paste.

Cut the chicken thighs in half. Put the pan in which the onions were cooked back on a medium heat. Add the bay leaf followed by the chicken pieces and seal both sides. Immediately pour the yoghurt mixture over the chicken and let the contents come to a boil. Cover, lower the heat and let it cook on a simmer. After 20 minutes, add the strips of orange rind to the chicken. Add the sugar and half the orange slices to the chicken at the very end.

Taste to check the seasoning and adjust as necessary.

When ready to serve, garnish with the remaining orange segments and the reserved fried lotus seeds.

Asma Khan is the chef and owner of Darjeeling Express in London; her books include Ammu: Indian Home-Cooking to Nourish Your Soul *and* Asma's Indian Kitchen

Dhruv Baker

SHIKAMPURI KABAB

Between the ages of five and 15, I lived in India and got to spend a lot of time with my mother's family. Some of my fondest memories from those years are of holidays in Limbdi, the home of my aunt and uncle, Bo and Lalji. They were times filled with laughter and happiness – and lots of food.

We would gather for family meals around a colossal table, laden with flavours that were new and exciting to my young and inquisitive palate. These were preceded by drinks, served on the veranda, with nibbles that were invariably more substantial that most meals. Often there was marinated game, grilled over charcoal, and sometimes these unbelievably soft and delicate lamb kababs.

The recipe comes from one of my most treasured cookbooks, which was written by my mother's uncle. The book is the wonderfully titled *Cooking Delights of the Maharajas*: Exotic Dishes from the *Princely House of Sailana* – a joy if you can get hold of a copy. In the book, the following line precedes the recipe: "I am grateful to His late Highness Maharajadhiraj Singhji of Kashmir for giving this fine recipe."

I have tweaked the heat level and salt content of the original kababs and removed the curd filling, as I grew up eating them without, but they are otherwise a true representation – and a reminder of those wondrous childhood days. They are best enjoyed outside at dusk on a summer's evening with a cold beer.

MAKES ABOUT 20 KABABS

1.5 litres water (or lamb/mutton/ hogget stock if you have it)

1kg lamb mince (mutton or hogget is far better if you can get it)

50g chana dal

2 tsp fine sea salt

4-5 whole dried Kashmiri chillies

2-4 whole fresh green chillies

5 black cardamom pods

5 dried bay leaves

5-6cm piece cassia bark

12 cloves

1 tsp ground garam masala

3-4 fresh green chillies, very finely chopped

3-4 tbsp fresh coriander, finely chopped

juice of 1 lime

200g thick yoghurt

2 eggs, whisked

vegetable oil for frying (about 75ml)

Pour the water or stock into a large pan and add the meat, chana dal, salt, red chillies, whole green chillies, black cardamom, bay leaves, cassia and cloves.

Bring to the boil and allow the water to cook off completely, stirring occasionally and taking care not to break the spices and chillies. This will take 1-1½ hours.

Once dry, remove and discard the whole spices, chillies and bay leaves.

Place the meat in a food processor, add the yoghurt, eggs, garam masala, chopped green chillies, coriander and lime juice. Switch on and run until the mixture is smooth. Refrigerate to firm up – a couple of hours is OK.

When firm enough to handle, form into patties of around 50-75g each (I use scales so they are all uniform; this avoids the inevitable squabbling about who got the biggest one). Wet your hands to keep the mixture from sticking. Place the kababs on a tray lined with baking parchment and refrigerate again for them to firm up (ideally overnight, but a couple of hours will suffice).

To cook, heat the oil in a large frying pan and fry on each side for 4-5 minutes till golden brown. Dry on kitchen roll and serve immediately.

Dhruv Baker is a chef, cookbook writer and founder of Tempus charcuterie

Sweet Things

Fergus Henderson

ÎLES FLOTTANTES

My deep love of all things sweet and romantic started when I discovered *îles flottantes*. I was 13 years old and in Paris with my best friend Ben. We both already shared a huge passion for food, having grown up with mothers who were keen cooks and Ben's stepmother being Ruthie Rogers. All were great inspirations for our cooking.

On this particular evening, we were wandering around Paris on a dessert discovery, guided by Ruthie. We had already eaten a miraculous chocolate cake, I remember. It was warm and the recipe was very much a secret. As the hunt continued, we arrived at some out-of-the-way little place, in Pigalle, I think. Ben and I both ordered the îles flottantes. It was incredible – love at first sight. In front of us was a perfect, beautiful floating island of poached meringue, a picture of softness and whiteness on a pool of custard, but caged by caramel, so it was unable to swim off. What a joy! Then the taste: gentle and soothing, with the caramel hitting a high note.

Back in London, I decided to try and make these islands myself. It would be the first recipe I ever followed, taken from *A Taste of France* by Caroline Conran. It was a memorable moment: gathering all the elements, the cooking, the coming together. It grabbed me and hooked me in. Maybe my passion for white food started here, too.

The recipe is still very dear to me. I love to see it float onto the menu at St John – my dear old friend, so glamorous and timeless, the perfect end to any meal. It suited me as a child and it still does: those mouthfuls that slip down so easily and just disappear. It doesn't come much saucier than that. No wonder this was the first recipe I followed. Emotional stuff.

SERVES 6

1.2 litres milk

2 vanilla pods, split and scraped

8 eggs

350g caster sugar

For the caramel

50g caster sugar

55ml water

Put the milk in a pan with the vanilla pods. Bring to a simmer and cook for 10 minutes.

Separate the eggs, yolks from whites. For the meringue, whisk together the egg whites and 275g of the sugar until they hold their shape. Shape gently into clouds and poach in the milk. Strain the milk into another pan.

For the custard, whisk the yolks with the remaining caster sugar. Add 250ml of the poaching milk, then return to the pan and allow to cook very gently until it thickens enough to coat a wooden spoon.

To make the caramel, melt the sugar and water in a pan until it turns a deep red-gold.

Pop your meringue onto the custard and tether it to the plate with a thin cage of caramel.

Fergus Henderson OBE is a chef, author and founder of St John restaurant in London. His books include Nose to Tail Eating

José Pizarro

CHURROS

Churros are treats that are world-famous – I haven't met a single person who doesn't love them. They bring so many fond memories to mind. Growing up in Cáceres in Andalucía, I usually had churros for breakfast as a child and can still remember waking up to the smell of the delicious dough being fried by my mum. Even now, whenever I smell them, I hear my mother saying "José, time to wake up! José, time for school!" It was such a delicious way to start the day.

Churros are also a celebratory treat – they are served at the ferias, the local Spanish festivals, or on New Year's Eve at the end of the night. Chocolate and churros are traditionally served as the last treat before guests head home.

Churros have always been part of my life and I'm so happy to be able to share my recipe with you. I hope it helps make many good memories for you too.

MAKES 20-25

- 250g plain flour
- 1 tsp baking powder
- a pinch of sea salt
- 320-350ml water
- 50ml extra virgin olive oil
- 1 litre olive oil or sunflower oil, for frying
- 50g caster sugar
- 1 tsp ground cinnamon

Sift the flour, baking powder and salt into a mixing bowl. Put the extra virgin olive oil and water into a saucepan and bring to the boil. Pour over the flour and beat until you have a thick but pipeable batter. Cover with clingfilm and chill for 20 minutes.

Heat the oil in a deep saucepan to 180C – or until a cube of bread browns in about 20 seconds. Fit a star nozzle to a large disposable piping bag and spoon the mixture into it. Once the oil is hot enough, pipe the mixture into the pan in long lines, using scissors to cut the batter when each churro is about 12cm long. Fry about three or four at a time for 3 minutes, until golden brown. Drain on kitchen paper.

Mix the sugar and cinnamon together in a shallow bowl and scatter over the top of the churros, or use to dip the ends into as you eat.

Serve with a nice thick chocolate and dip the churros. There are lots of different brands of chocolate but you just need to make sure it's really thick, almost like a chocolate pot.

José Pizarro is a chef with several restaurants in London, including Pizarro, and José Pizarro at RA. His books include The Spanish Home Kitchen *and* Andalusia: Recipes from Seville and Beyond

Anna Jones

SOUR CHERRY AND
VANILLA WELSH CAKES

Some families have a wealth of handed-down recipes, carefully written out in notebooks with welcome splatters and curling corners. My family does not. My dad is one of 12 brothers and sisters, so my nan (or mam) didn't have time to go to the corner shop, let alone write down a recipe.

On my mum's Irish, Catholic side, there was just my grandma, and while she and my mum both loved food, their life in a bedsit on a budget meant neither of them were keen cooks. My only food inheritance was simple Sunday roasts, egg and chips and the odd treat: chocolate bars, fruit pies and – my favourite – Welsh cakes, either made by my aunties or bought from the shop.

The Welsh cakes I grew up with were dotted with raisins or currants and flavoured with a hint of mixed spice. But recipes to me are like a food tapestry, with new threads being added as the old ones fray, and I've taken liberties with the original, updating it with vanilla, lemon and lime and fat sour cherries – flavours I now love.

The cakes are best eaten warmed in the oven (though the toaster also does a good job) with cups of milky tea. And preferably aunties.

350g plain flour

2 tsp baking powder

175g unsalted butter or dairy-
free spread

115g golden caster sugar, plus
extra for dusting

100g sour cherries

1 vanilla pod, seeds scraped out,
or 1 tsp vanilla bean paste

zest of 1 unwaxed lemon

zest of 1 unwaxed lime

sea salt

1 egg, beaten

2-3 tbsp milk

Sift the flour and baking powder into a bowl. Use your fingertips to rub in the butter or dairy-free spread until the mixture resembles breadcrumbs, then mix in the sugar, sour cherries, vanilla, citrus zests and a pinch of salt. Mix in the beaten egg and 2 tablespoons of the milk, then bring together with your hands to form a firm dough. If it seems a bit dry, add another tablespoon of milk.

Lightly flour a clean work surface and roll out the dough to about 1cm thick. Use a 6cm round cutter to stamp out circles, bringing the dough back together and recutting until it has all been used up.

Heat a large, heavy frying pan or flat griddle over a low heat (no need to add any oil) and cook the Welsh cakes five at a time. This should give you plenty of room to flip them over and will ensure they cook evenly. Cook for 2-3 minutes each side, until deep golden.

Cool the cakes on a wire rack, then dust with caster sugar and a little salt. Eat warm on the day you make them, either on their own or with butter and jam.

Anna Jones is a chef and food writer. She is the author of cookbooks including One: Pot, Pan, Planet *and writes regularly for* The Guardian *and* Observer Food Monthly

PEAR AND GINGER CAKE

You could cut the atmosphere with a cake knife. Mum trying her best to read the map, my dad too embarrassed to admit we were well and truly lost among the winding country lanes. I sat in the back of the car, sulking, thinking about the rapidly disappearing afternoon tea we had set out for.

"Stop, Daddy, stop!" I yelled as I spotted a sign bearing the legend of my dreams. "Devon Cream Teas. Open." I don't know which one of us was the most relieved to get out of the car.

As we sat outside, the wind was up, and we had to hold on to our paper napkins to stop them blowing away. There was a Brown Betty pot of tea for Mum and Dad, lemon barley water for me, a basket of scones with little dishes of jam and cream and a plate of brown bread and butter. Best of all there was cake. Thick wedges of cream sponge and three slices of gingerbread, dark as night, whose tacky surface stuck to your fingers. There is something rather grown up about gingerbread to an eight-year-old boy. Especially when it comes decorated with a coin of spicy crystallised ginger, like an amber jewel.

Mum ate a slice of sponge with its snow of icing sugar, Dad had ginger cake. I had both. As we paid and left, my father complimented the kindly owner on her tea and chatted briefly about the view of the surrounding fields and hedges. (I distinctly remember my parents being obsessed with "views". We would travel miles just to sit in the car and gaze out at the scenery.) "I don't suppose," my father said somewhat sheepishly, "I could trouble you for the ginger cake recipe?" The woman's face changed in a heartbeat. She looked down at her flowery apron, shook her head, and gently but firmly said, "No, I'm sorry."

My dad nodded a goodbye without smiling and we clambered back in the car. Mum said what a lovely tea it had been. My dad was less enthused, openly hurt by the owner's refusal to reveal her recipe.

I never forgot that cake. Neither did I forget the look of quiet hurt on my father's face. Over the years I made several attempts at recreating that ginger cake in the hope of reproducing that memorable slice of heaven. Alas, the results were always a little too heavy, sometimes too pale and never, ever moist enough. And then I got the dark muscovado sugar out. I added some butter-fried pears to the mixture too and came up with what is probably my favourite cake.

Of course, it was a little late for my father, who was no longer with us by that time, but my memory of that day, the view across the Devon countryside, the scones and jam and that gorgeous slice of cake seems somehow all the more vivid when I have a piece of my own pear-and-ginger cake on my plate.

For the pears

500g pears, peeled, cored, diced

30g butter

1 tbsp agave or golden syrup

For the cake

250g self-raising flour

2 level tsp ground ginger

½ tsp mixed spice

½ tsp ground cinnamon

1 tsp bicarbonate of soda

pinch of salt

200ml agave or golden syrup

125g butter

125g dark muscovado

2 large eggs

240ml milk

For the icing

250g icing sugar

3 tbsp lemon juice

3 knobs preserved ginger in syrup

1 tbsp demerara or golden sugar crystals

1 tbsp poppy seeds

You will need a square cake tin measuring approximately 22cm.

Peel, halve and core the pears, then cut them into 2cm dice. Warm the butter in a shallow, non-stick pan, then add the pears and leave to cook for 10 minutes over a low to moderate heat, until pale gold and translucent. Towards the end of their cooking time, add the agave or golden syrup. Remove from the heat and set aside.

Line the base and sides of the cake tin with baking parchment.Set the oven at 180C/160C Fan/Gas 4.

Sift the flour with the ground ginger, mixed spice, cinnamon, bicarbonate of soda and salt. Pour the syrup into a small saucepan, add the butter and the muscovado and warm over a moderate heat until the butter has melted. When the mixture has simmered for a minute, remove from the heat.

Break the eggs into a bowl, add the milk and beat lightly to combine. Pour the butter and syrup mixture into the flour and spices and stir gently until no flour is visible. Mix in the milk and eggs. Fold in the cooked pears and scrape the mixture into the lined cake tin. The pears should sink to the bottom. Slide the cake into the oven and bake for about 35-40 minutes, until it is lightly puffed and spongy to the touch. Leave to cool in the tin.

To make the icing, put the icing sugar into a bowl, then beat in the lemon juice, either with a fork or using a small hand whisk. Take it steady, only using enough to make an icing thick enough that it takes a while to fall from the spoon.

Remove the cake from its tin and peel back the parchment. Cut the cake into 16 equal pieces and place them on a cooling rack set over a tray. Trickle the icing over the cakes, letting a little run down the sides of each. When the icing is almost set, add a slice of crystallised ginger and a scattering of sugar crystals and poppy seeds.

Nigel Slater OBE is a food writer, columnist for The Observer, *broadcaster and author of several best-selling cookbooks, diaries and memoirs, including* Greenfeast, A Cook's Book *and* Toast: A Story of a Boy's Hunger

Lisa Markwell

SPICED EXOTIC FRUIT

There was a rustling sound as a small hand reached into my bag and brought out a lychee. My newly adopted daughter, just four, had never had much fresh fruit and certainly nothing exotic like this. As she watched, agog, I peeled the curious skin and removed the stone. I let her nibble the flesh and she laughed...

We sometimes forget the privilege of good food, but that moment set in train a determination in me (a new and extremely underprepared parent) to give my children the gift of edible exploration. Everything was new and even though there were some refusals, on the whole they adored discoveries – so much so that they both became brilliant restaurant-review companions. My daughter once slipped away from the table at a Peter Gordon restaurant and helpfully told the kitchen staff, "My mum's Lisa Markwell and she is reviewing your restaurant", which, I suspect, led to very generous portions and attentive service.

The giddy pleasure of sweet, sultry, soft fruit has never changed and even when little, this dish of exotic treats spiked with flavour-intensifying aromatics was regularly called for. It is not a dish to serve with cream, but a soothing sorbet could be on hand in case of a little too much heat.

120g caster sugar

1 Scotch bonnet chilli (use milder if you like)

6 black peppercorns

2 star anise

1 vanilla pod, split lengthways

1 lemon

1 mango

1 papaya

1 small pineapple

8 lychees

1-2 passionfruit (you could also use persimmons, bananas, Charentais melon etc, whatever you like and can find)

Heat the sugar, chilli, peppercorns, star anise and vanilla pod in a small saucepan with 3 strips of lemon peel (use a vegetable peeler) and 250ml water. Allow to come to a simmer, check that all the sugar has dissolved then cook at a low simmer for a further 10 minutes. Remove from the heat and add the lemon juice.

While the syrup is simmering, peel all the fruit and slice the mango, papaya, pineapple (or whichever fruit you're using) in chunks or slices, as you prefer. Place in a pretty bowl.

Immediately pour over the still-warm syrup (I leave in the chilli and spices, but you can sieve them out), then halve and scoop out the passionfruit seeds and mix everything together.

Serve on its own at room temperature or chilled, or with thin gingersnaps or a mint/lime sorbet.

Lisa Markwell is a food writer, journalist and private chef, who currently edits The Telegraph's Weekend *magazine*

Claire Ptak

GLUTEN-FREE TEFF BANANA CRUMBLE LOAF

Summer weekends in Inverness, California, were protracted, endless episodes that cut between the dusty beach and the forest that surrounded it and our treetop home. Often alone in the afternoons after a swim in the bay with friends, with my older brother doing older brother things and my parents working their second, weekend jobs, I'd find something to bake.

There was one store in our town, aptly called The Inverness Store. It sold beach balls and colourful plastic buckets and shovels for making sand castles alongside an amazing candy selection, a video rental section, Campbell's canned foods, a few vegetables, baking essentials and a rack of bread from various suppliers. The bread rack also housed a few industrially produced cakes.

It was the banana crumble cake that I loved the most. Moist and fragrant with bananas, and with a buttery, almost shortbread-like crumble topping. I rarely had enough money to buy it, so I tried my best to figure out how to make it myself. We always had bananas and flour and sugar at home. The version here is healthier, with whole-grain gluten-free flours and, to me, tastes better.

I've tried to find that cake a few times since, but it doesn't exist, even online. Did I make it up? Did I imagine those flavours together? Does it matter? Baking was always a way to feel connected when I was growing up. I did it instinctively and habitually. It kept me company, like only a good cake can.

For the banana bread

600g banana (about 400g
    without the skins)

120g vegetable oil

200g dark brown sugar

1 tbsp vanilla extract

1 tsp rum

2 eggs

80g plain yoghurt

1 tsp bicarbonate of soda

1 tsp baking powder

140g teff flour

35g tapioca flour

35g brown rice flour

1 tsp xanthan gum

½ tsp salt

For the crumble topping

50g teff flour

50g walnuts

50g caster sugar

pinch of sea salt

150g unsalted butter, cold, cut
    into cubes

Preheat the oven to 190C/170C Fan/Gas 5. Grease a large 900g loaf tin and line with parchment paper.

Add the banana, oil, brown sugar, vanilla, rum, eggs and yoghurt to the bowl of an electric mixer and mix with the paddle attachment. You can also do this by hand using a spoon to break up the bananas.

In a separate bowl, stir together the dry ingredients, then add to the wet ingredients and mix until just combined. Be careful not to overmix or your bread will be tough. Allow the mixture to sit for 15 minutes to allow the flours to combine fully.

Meanwhile, prepare the crumble topping. Put all the crumble ingredients in a food processor and pulse until you get a sandy texture, but not so much that it forms a dough. Keep a close eye.

Give the banana mix a final stir and tip it into the prepared baking dish. Sprinkle evenly with the crumble mixture.

Bake straight away in your preheated oven for 55-65 minutes or until set in the middle.

Allow to cool for at least 45 minutes before slicing.

Claire Ptak is a baker, food writer and founder of Violet Cakes in London

Simon Hopkinson

RICE PUDDING

Ahhh... lovely rice pudding. Among all the dredge of memories that make me happy about food, rice pudding was my first time of knowing and seeing exactly what I wanted to eat. "Only pudding, Mummy," I pointed impatiently, spoilt indulged child that I was. "I want only pudding!" And so, the ancient hotel dining room trolley came trundling over, guided by someone I would now describe as – how shall we say? – matronly.

"He just wants that," my mother said. "Only the rice pudding. No jam. Just some of the creamy part and a bit of the skin, but not the burnt bits..." Politely interjected into this needy scenario, I am sure, would have been the occasional "please" and "thank you so much". My well-mannered mother would never have wanted to come across as intentionally discourteous – though she did have a particular "smile" that could flatten one with its forced geniality.

I was four years old and I liked that I was being indulged. And I did get that perfect serving from the large, oval glass dish (surely it must have been Pyrex?). And I remember it was just that: a slightly rumpled, dark golden baked skin at the centre, together with surrounding creamy bits. Two big spoonfuls, just for me.

Forever more, in our house, rice pudding would be known as "only pudding".

SERVES 4

40g butter
75g caster sugar
100g pudding rice (or Spanish paella rice)
1 vanilla pod, split lengthways
1 litre full cream milk
150ml double cream
large pinch of salt
plenty of freshly grated nutmeg

Preheat the oven to 150C/130C Fan/Gas 2.

Melt the butter in a solid-based casserole and add the sugar. Stir and heat gently until gooey, then add the rice and vanilla pod, and continue stirring until the rice looks a touch puffed and is sticky with sugar. Now, gently pour in the milk, which will seethe around the rice causing the volatile mixture to set into lumps. However, fear not, for as you stir around in this milky mess any sugary lumps will soon dissolve into the milk as it heats up. Continuing to stir, add the cream and salt, and bring to a simmer.

Give it a final stir and grate about a third of a small nutmeg over the surface (do not stir again). Pop in the oven and bake for about an hour or so. Once there is a nice, thin tarpaulin-like skin on the surface (a touch burnished if you like) and the pudding only just wobbles in the centre, it is ready to remove. Remember, the rice will continue cooking further as the heat wanes within.

Serve warm, or at room temperature.

Simon Hopkinson is a chef, food writer, broadcaster and author of several best-selling books, including Roast Chicken and Other Stories

Itamar Srulovich

PEACH BICI BICI

As children growing up in Jerusalem, we always knew where to find the *malabi* sellers.
They were an institution, their kiosks and wooden carts dotted through the cobbled
alleyways of the old city. They would make the *malabi* to order, scooping milk jelly into
disposable cups from a chilled metal container, drizzling it with sweet rosewater syrup and
sprinkling the top with desiccated coconut or powdered cinnamon. We would retreat to a
shady corner and savour the combination of tooth-melting sweetness and milky whiteness, a
cooling treat in the heat of summer.

Malabi was introduced to Israel from Turkey and it was there, a few years ago, that I
was transported back to those childhood moments. We were in Adana in the south of the
country, a place where summer temperatures regularly top 40C. By late morning, the air felt
heavy on the skin.

People have found various ways to beat the punishing heat, sitting in the park next to the
river or grabbing a table under a tree in one of the cafés by the dam, where the gushing water
cools the air. But by far the tastiest way to stay cool in this part of the world is with an icy
dessert, bought, like the *malabi* of my youth, from brightly coloured handcarts. Shaved ice,
glistening like glass, is piled into a cup, along with cool, translucent cubes of set jelly,
a squeeze of lemon and a generous pouring of achingly sweet rose syrup. This cooling snow
cone is a perfect tonic for the heat and has the most delicious name: *bici bici* (pronounced
be-chi be-chi).

Here in London, it is now our favourite dessert. It's a doddle to make and the variations
are endless. The peach version below is, I think, the tastiest and rolls off the tongue so well
– peach *bici bici*. Make the jelly with a delicate floral infusion, such as chamomile or jasmine.
Both will work well with the peach snow to make a light, cooling summertime dessert.
It may not get as hot as in southern Turkey, but summer is summer and life should be peachy
(*bici bici*).

SERVES 6

For the peach ice

250g orange-fleshed peaches
(about 2 large ones)

1 heaped tbsp icing sugar

For the chamomile base

2 tbsp dried chamomile or 2
bags of chamomile tea

500ml boiling water

30g cornflour

1 tbsp honey

For the roasted peaches

500g flat white peaches (5-6),
each cut into 6 wedges

100g caster sugar

juice of 1 lemon

Start by making the peach ice. Peel the peaches, cut away the stone, then place the flesh with the sugar and 2 tablespoons of water in a food processor and purée until they are completely smooth. Transfer to a small tray and place in the freezer for at least 4 hours.

Make the chamomile pudding by infusing the chamomile in the hot water, add the honey and stir well to dissolve. Rest and infuse until the mix has entirely cooled. Strain through a fine sieve and use 50ml of the infusion to dissolve the cornflour. Place the rest in a small saucepan on the stove and bring to a boil.

As soon as it has boiled, add the liquid cornflour in a steady stream, stirring constantly, until the entire mix thickens and comes back to a boil. Pour out into a flat tray and set aside to firm up for about 15 minutes, then pour over 2-3 tablespoons of cold water to form a thin layer on the top of the pudding to avoid it forming a skin. Place in the fridge to fully set for at least 3 hours.

Heat your oven to 200C/180C Fan/Gas 6 and mix the peaches with the sugar and lemon juice. Place in the oven and roast for 6-8 minutes, depending on the softness of your peaches. The sugar should all be dissolved and the peaches should feel soft to the touch, but still holding their shape. Cool a little then place in the fridge.

When you are ready to serve, cut out a wedge of the chamomile pudding and place it in a bowl, top with some roasted peaches and a couple of spoonfuls of the syrup they have formed. Remove the block of peach ice from the freezer and grate it or scrape it off with a firm spoon. Top the peaches with the ice and serve immediately

Itamar Srulovich is a chef and co-founder, with Sarit Packer, of Honey & Co, Honey & Spice and Honey & Smoke in London. A version of this story first appeared in **The Financial Times**

David Loftus

MOLLY WRIGGLESWORTH'S APPLE PIE

Mary Florence Wrigglesworth – known to us as Auntie Molly – was a Miss Potteresque character, a cross between Mary Poppins and Mrs Tiggy-Winkle. She was born in Ryhope, County Durham, in 1922 and, at the age of eight, was present, with towels and hot water, at the birth of my mother. Thirty years later, she was there again, this time when my mother gave birth first to my identical twin, Johnny, and, 10 minutes later, to me.

Molly spent her whole life looking after others, particularly the Loftus family, who she saw through births, Christmasses, christenings, unfortunate events, sickness, marriages and, tragically, the deaths of both my father and my twin. An excellent and knowledgeable cook, she would rustle up a stir-fry or Yorkshire pudding with gravy as the situation required, though best of all was her apple pie, which was accompanied by a never-ending supply of cups (never mugs) of tea and hot buttered toast. The pie was a comforting life saver and, having discovered I had an account with a local courier firm, she would often bike beautifully packed slices to my twin to raise his spirits.

Molly finally hung up her pinny when she was 90. This recipe is adapted from her scrapbook.

For the pastry

300g plain flour

2 tbsp granulated sugar

1 tbsp Maldon salt

175g unsalted butter, cut into
    1cm cubes & softened

3-4 tbsp of iced water

For the filling

150g light brown sugar

3 tbsp plain flour

½ tsp ground cinnamon

⅓ tsp ground nutmeg

½ tsp ground cardamom

a pinch of ground ginger

a pinch of Maldon salt

1kg Granny Smith apples,
    peeled, cored and sliced

1 tbsp fresh lemon juice

For the top

1½ tbsp unsalted butter, melted
    (or a beaten egg)

2 tbsp caster sugar

To serve

good quality vanilla ice cream

Preheat the oven to 200C/180C Fan/Gas 6.

To make the pastry, sift the flour, sugar and salt into a medium-sized bowl.

Add the softened butter and mix together (using your hands, a fork or a food processor) until fully, but coarsely combined.

Slowly add the iced water, bit by bit, stirring until the dough firms up. Go on instinct here, adding a little more water if the dough feels too dry. Cover with clingfilm and pop in the fridge for later.

Now for the filling. Put the brown sugar, flour, cinnamon, nutmeg, cardamom, salt and ginger in a mixing bowl and mix away. In a separate bowl, toss your slices of apple with the lemon juice, then gradually add the sugar-and-spice-and-all-things-nice mixture, stirring well with a metal spoon until the apples are evenly coated.

Lightly flour a clean, smooth work surface. Take the dough from the fridge and roll it out into a 40cm circle, big enough to blanket a 23cm pie dish. Dust the surface with flour and gently lay the dough over the dish, using your fingers to press it carefully into the edges. Allow the excess to hang over the sides.

Fill the pie dish with your slices of spiced apple and fold the dough up and over the filling in Tiggy-Winkle fashion. It should look higgledy-piggledy and shouldn't reach the middle.

Brush the top with melted butter or beaten egg and sprinkle with caster sugar. Bake for about 45 minutes, or until the crust is golden brown, as the Stranglers once sang, and the apples are a tender, treacly, spiced delight. Serve in your finest pinny with scoops of vanilla ice cream.

David Loftus is a leading food photographer, who has worked with many chefs and food writers including Jamie Oliver, Nigella Lawson, Heston Blumenthal and Gordon Ramsay

Darina Allen

CARRAGEEN MOSS PUDDING WITH SWEET GERANIUM

This is so good, I weaned my kids on it. Myrtle Allen introduced me to carrageen moss when I became a member of the Ballymaloe House family by the simple expedient of marrying the boss's son in 1970. When I understood that it was made from seaweed, I was properly wary. Surely it must taste weird or at least salty? But everyone at Ballymaloe seemed to love it and I didn't want to appear unsophisticated, so I plucked up the courage. Such a surprise: a delicate flavour, the texture of junket and irresistible with a blob of softly whipped cream and a sprinkling of soft brown sugar. I grew to love it so much that I chose carrageen moss pudding and fraughans (wild bilberries) for our wedding feast at Ballymaloe House.

For years, Myrtle bought carrageen moss from Fred Dawes and his wife, a wonderful old couple who collected it off the rocks in the little bay of Ballyandreen, east of Ballycotton in Co. Cork. They passed on the secret to Myrtle who showed me how to identify, harvest and cure the little seaweed. She was determined to pass on the skill and knowledge of what she considered, as do I, to be an important part of our traditional food culture.

Carrageen (*Chondrus crispus*) is a superfood if ever there was one. It enables your metabolism to work to its optimum, and breaks down fats. Years ago, people fed it to racehorses and greyhounds to give them strength and energy without putting on weight – jockeys also know its value.

Carrageen means "little rock" in Gaelic. It's a low-growing seaweed, a red algae that can be found in abundance around the coast of Ireland. In its natural form, it is purpley-brown in colour. We harvest it after the spring tides every year. Traditionally it is laid out on the soft spongy grass on the top of the cliffs where it is regularly turned, washed by the rain and bleached by the sun for up to 10 days. When it is dry, it will keep forever and is a brilliant vitamin-, iodine- and sulphur-rich food. We all love it, although many people have less than fond memories of carrageen moss, partly because some recipes call for far too much carrageen. It has a very strong natural gelatine, so the trick is to use little enough.

This recipe is a riff on the original, given to me by Myrtle Allen, and is by far the most delicious I know. I've infused the base with sweet geranium, which perfumes the base with a haunting lemony flavour. Nowadays, a growing number of chefs are using carrageen on their menus but often they add stronger flavours such as treacle or rosewater, which tend to mask the delicate flavour of the carrageen itself. Carrageen moss is served at Ballymaloe House every night on the famous Ballymaloe sweet trolley.

SERVES 6-8

8g cleaned, well-dried carrageen moss (1 semi-closed fistful)

900ml whole milk

8 medium leaves of sweet geranium

1 vanilla pod, optional

1 large egg, preferably free-range

1 tbsp caster sugar

To serve

soft brown sugar and cream

6-8 frosted sweet geranium leaves

Soak the carrageen in tepid water for 10 minutes. Strain off the water and put the carrageen and sweet geranium into a saucepan with the milk and vanilla, if using. Bring to the boil and simmer gently, lid on, for 20 minutes.

At that point, and not before, separate the egg and put the yolk into a bowl. Add the sugar and whisk together for a few seconds. Pour the milk, carrageen and sweet geranium through a strainer onto the egg yolk mixture, whisking all the time. The carrageen will now be swollen and exuding jelly. Rub all this jelly through the strainer and beat it into the liquid.

Test for a set in a cold saucer: put it in the fridge and it should set in a couple of minutes. Rub a little more through the strainer if necessary. Whisk the egg white until stiff peaks form and fold it in gently; it will rise to make a fluffy top. Leave to cool.

Serve chilled with softly whipped cream and frosted sweet geranium leaves.

Edible flowers and leaves crystallised with sugar will keep for months. The end result is both beautiful and rewarding. Smaller flowers are more attractive when crystallised, e.g. primroses, violets, apple blossom, violas, rose petals. Use fairly strong textured leaves, such as sweet geranium, mint, lemon balm, sweet cicely, wild strawberry, salad burnet or marguerite daisy.

The caster sugar must be absolutely dry – one could dry it in a low oven for about 30 minutes.

Break up the egg white slightly in a bowl with a fork. Using a child's paintbrush, paint the egg white carefully over each petal and into every crevice. Pour the caster sugar over the flower with a teaspoon. Arrange the flowers on silicone paper so that they retain a good shape. Leave to dry overnight in a warm, dry place such as close to an Aga, over a radiator or in an airing cupboard. We store them in a pottery jar or a tin box with an airtight lid.

Darina Allen is a chef, writer, broadcaster and founder of the Ballymaloe Cookery School in Ireland. Her books include Forgotten Skills of Cooking *and* How to Cook

SWEET GERANIUM.

Pelargonium graveolens

Chantal Coady

BUCKWHEAT PANCAKES, BANANAS AND CHOCOLATE SAUCE

Pancakes have been an integral part of my life for as long as I can remember. My father believed a healthy breakfast was an essential start to the day. His solution was to take one egg and stretch it with milk and flour, making a pancake batter that would feed five children, served with lemons and sugar, and cooked by my long-suffering mother, who seemed happy to stand there cooking each of us a pancake before we headed off to school.

A holiday in Brittany gave us all a taste for galettes, the savoury pancakes made from buckwheat, and these days I use buckwheat flour whenever I can. It's not only gluten-free, but you can cook the batter immediately, unlike traditional wheat flour, which needs to stand for hours before you use it. I often have them for Sunday lunch, accompanied by a crumbly white cheese such as Wensleydale with mango chutney and lime pickle, but other times I serve them with chopped bananas and a simple chocolate sauce.

Chocolate was my passion before it became my career and, as a hungry convent girl, I climbed through the windows of the domestic science lab to make pancakes, which I ate with grated cooking chocolate from the cupboard. The pleasure of these illicit treats brings back memories of teenage rebellion – especially sweet as I never got caught.

Here is the pancake recipe, adapted from the one in my old exercise book, as taught by Mrs Chalmers, who I remember being very fierce. It has now become a staple for the next generation of my family.

For the banana version, you can either put the chopped bananas straight into the buttery pan before pouring on the batter, or slice them raw onto a cooked pancake and cover with the chocolate sauce. A bit of crème fraîche would not go amiss.

SERVES 4

115g flour (plain or buckwheat)

pinch of salt

1 large egg

285ml milk

butter, melted

a bar of the best dark
  chocolate you can find

Sift the flour and salt together into a bowl and make a well in the middle. Break the eggs into the well and add a little of the milk. Mix to a creamy consistency with a wooden spoon.

Beat well, for about 5 minutes, then add the remainder of the milk. Pour into a jug and chill in the fridge for 30 minutes (or even overnight if using wheat flour).

Brush a hot, non-stick frying pan with a bit of melted butter and swirl in enough of the pancake batter to thinly coat the bottom. Cook until golden underneath, then turn or flip and cook for a minute or so more.

For the chocolate sauce, break the chocolate into small pieces, put in a heavy-bottomed pan and add the same weight of freshly boiled water. Allow the chocolate to melt and whisk it while very gently heating until it becomes thick and glossy, then pour over your pancakes.

Chantal Coady OBE is a chocolatier, founder of The Chocolate Detective and Rococo, and author of several books on chocolate, including Rococo: Mastering the Art of Chocolate

Anna Del Conte

LEMON GRANITA

I grew up at Number 3 Via Gesù in the centre of Milan. It was a pleasant 19th-century house that had been divided into four large flats. The attic used to house the maids' bedrooms and was icy cold in winter and sweltering hot in summer, but it had a spectacular view of the roof and chimneys of the house next door – the Palazzo Bagatti-Valsecchi – which is now a museum. The palazzo is a very large building, lavishly built in Gothic style – a bit of a mish-mash, but quite attractive. Its roofs are splendid, all set at different angles.

I'd go up to the attic every October to see the swallows gathering in the sky before they left for warmer shores. I envied them, as I hated the cold and the grey of northern climes. But then the snow would come and the attic became so appealing again. I'd sprinkle breadcrumbs for the birds – the house martins and the sparrows. I did it religiously every day as soon as I got back from school, and I used to think how silly Hansel and Gretel were to sprinkle breadcrumbs in a forest as a route marker. No wonder they couldn't find their way home. It snowed a lot in northern Italy then; now, apparently, it seldom lies for more than two or three days. The roofs and the chimney pots of the Palazzo Bagatti-Valsecchi would become a good foot higher, thanks to that lovely crunchy white snow.

Another sortie to the attic was for our winter treat: lemon granita. My brother Guido and I would get two tall glasses from the kitchen, pour quite a lot of freshly squeezed lemon juice into them, sprinkle in an even greater amount of sugar and mix and mix, and up we went to the attic. We'd open the window and fill the glasses with that cold white crunchy manna. Then back down to the kitchen, where we'd squeeze more lemon juice, sprinkle more sugar and slowly suck the granita up. The best drink ever, even in the depths of winter.

SERVES 2

180g sugar

400ml water

100ml lemon juice

Put the sugar and water in a small saucepan and bring to the boil. Simmer for 5 minutes, then mix in the lemon juice and leave to cool.

When cold, pour into a freezer container, seal and place in the freezer. Leave it there for at least 4 hours, stirring it with a fork every 20 minutes or so to break up any ice lumps that form.

Anna Del Conte is a cook, food writer and author of many books on Italian food, including Portrait of Pasta *and* The Gastronomy of Italy

Alison Elliott

FLORENCE VARLEY'S HONEY CAKE

When I was growing up my father kept bees at the bottom of the garden. He was too tight to buy a bee suit and would disappear off dressed in an antique top hat with a veil made from old tulle and some motorcycle boots for protection. This did little to encourage my participation in the actual beekeeping, so the closest I got was helping to bake my grandmother's honey cake, a recipe that is like no other for the pure quantity of honey in the ingredients.

You could argue that any cake with honey in it is bound to be delicious. It is one of those beguilingly simple loaf cakes that we ate for breakfast, for elevenses, that was often a bit of a disappointment in my packed lunch when everybody else had a KitKat, but was excellent after school or for pudding with a dollop of cream. To make it, the ingredients are melted, mixed and poured into a tin – a method that as a child I quickly mastered on my own.

Honey cake continued to arrive in the post long after I had left home until finally, a few years ago, my father decided that the bees were getting too much for him. The night came when we drove to my parents' house with a big roll of clingfilm, wrapped up his three sleeping hives, put them in the boot of the car and drove home. We became beekeepers overnight and the mantle of honey-cake baking transferred back to me.

Our honey has a very different flavour to the one of my childhood – the well-tended, flower-filled gardens of 1980s suburbia provided a more varied menu for the bees than the woodland around us now. But our strong, slightly bitter chestnut honey makes the cake even more fragrant and honeyed than before.

Serve it, as my grandmother Florence Varley did, with a glass of Amontillado instead of afternoon tea. This will see you safely through till supper.

My mum used to make it in a massive old loaf tin, but I use the same recipe to make a 2lb cake and a 1lb cake. I give the small cake away, even though in fact it is never quite as good as the large one.

140ml milk

2 large eggs

575g honey

225g butter

350g plain flour

2 tsp bicarbonate of soda

Butter a 2lb/900g loaf tin and a 1lb/450g tin and line the base and sides of both with strips of baking parchment. Preheat the oven to 150C/130C Fan/Gas 2.

Sift the flour and bicarbonate of soda into a mixing bowl.

Put the butter and honey in a saucepan and melt over a low heat. Leave to cool.

Beat the eggs, add the milk, then stir in the butter and honey mix.

Make a well in the flour mix and – gradually – add the batter. The whole thing takes no more than 5 minutes.

Pour into the prepared tins and bake for 1¼ hours (that's the 2lb cake – the 1lb cake takes an hour). Run a palette knife around the edge, then leave to cool before turning out.

It should be left for at least a day before eating to get nice and moist.

Alison Elliott is the co-owner of the Ham & Cheese Company, which imports artisan charcuterie and cheese from Italy and the Pays Basque

Edd Kimber

MY NANNA'S GINGERBREAD

In my parents' kitchen sits a little box stuffed full of handwritten recipes and pages ripped from old food magazines. Its contents form something akin to a family history. There is the cheesecake recipe written at the end of a telegram sent to my mother from her cousin in Australia, the "Canadian chocolate cake" recipe brought back from cousins in Vancouver when my mum was a teenager and many other gems. But among this collection of notes and torn-out pages, one is extra special – this recipe for gingerbread, jotted down by my maternal grandmother, probably 50 years ago (though the recipe is much older).

My Nanna passed away when I was just a toddler and my memories of her are really just regurgitated stories, told to me over the years by other family members. But whenever I make this cake, something I do quite often, I think about her and the tales I grew up hearing. It's as if the recipe is my connection to her, a stand-in for the memories I was never able to make as a child, and it is something I will hold onto forever – a link not only to my past, but to my family today.

170g plain flour

170g plain wholemeal flour

3 tsp ground ginger

1 tsp mixed spice

1 tsp ground cinnamon

1 tsp bicarbonate of soda

½ tsp fine sea salt

pinch of cayenne pepper

170g unsalted butter

115g caster sugar

2 tbsp orange marmalade

2 tbsp diced candied stem
    ginger

340g golden syrup

2 large eggs

210ml whole milk

Preheat the oven to 150C/130C Fan/Gas 2. Lightly grease a deep 20cm square cake tin and line with parchment paper.

Place all the dry ingredients into a large bowl and whisk together to combine. Place the butter, sugar, marmalade, stem ginger and golden syrup into a saucepan and cook over a medium heat until everything has melted together and you have a smooth mixture. Remove from the heat and allow to cool slightly before mixing in the milk, followed by the eggs.

Pour the liquid mixture into the bowl of dry ingredients and whisk together briefly until a smooth cake batter is formed. If you whisk too much it can become a little tough, so err on the side of caution. Pour the finished batter into the prepared tin and bake in the preheated oven for about 60-80 minutes or until the cake springs back to a light touch or a skewer inserted into the middle comes out clean. Allow to cool for 20 minutes before turning out onto a wire rack to cool completely.

As with all gingerbread cakes, this recipe will be even better if you can resist cutting into it for a couple days. The flavours improve and the cake becomes a little stickier, so hold back from trying it if you can – though I won't blame you if the smell out of the oven is too much to resist.

Edd Kimber is a baker and winner of the first ever Great British Bake Off. *His several cookbooks include* The Boy Who Bakes *and* One Tin Bakes

Richard Bertinet

FAR BRETON

I grew up in Quiberon, a beautiful seaside town in the south of Brittany, and Far Breton is something I've eaten for as long as I can remember. It's an ancient Breton dish – like a cross between crème caramel, crème brûlée, flan and creamy custard, dotted with rum-soaked prunes that add warmth and texture. The name comes from the Latin for flour – farina.

When I was growing up, there would always be a dish of far in the kitchen to snack on when we got home from school. It was the most welcome of treats, particularly on dark February afternoons, and there would invariably be a battle for the last slice. I remember sneaking a few prunes from the bowl as they soaked in rum. It was too much for a young boy and after three or four, I felt more than a little tipsy.

My mother got her recipe from my grandmother, who would make it for us when we went to visit. My mum, in turn, passed it on to me, though the transfer wasn't entirely straightforward. When I asked for the measurements, I realised the only measuring device my mum ever used was a half-burnt wooden spoon.

Far is an adaptable thing. It can be made with sultanas or caramelised apples instead of prunes, and you can serve it fresh, just a couple of hours after baking, or cold from the fridge. Either way, trust me – it won't last long.

250g prunes, stoned

50g rum

50g unsalted butter, melted, for greasing

130g caster sugar

220g egg (shelled weight): roughly equivalent to 4 large eggs

110g plain white flour

a pinch of salt

750g cold full fat milk

Soak the prunes in the rum for a few hours, or overnight if possible. Preheat the oven to 220C/200C Fan/Gas 7.

Grease a 20 x 25cm or equivalent deep (about 4cm) oval earthenware dish. Brush with the melted butter and put in the oven to warm for 1-2 minutes.

Mix the sugar and eggs together and gradually add the flour then the salt. Whisk in the cold milk bit by bit to make a thin batter. Spoon the prunes into your buttered dish, then put in the oven for a few minutes to warm. Remove from the oven and pour in the batter.

Bake in the oven for 10 minutes, then turn down the heat to 180C/160C Fan/Gas 4 and bake for 25-30 minutes more. Dip the blade of a sharp knife into cold water, then use it to pierce the middle – if the knife comes out clean, the far is ready. The sides will also be starting to come away from the dish. Cool completely, before cutting into slices. Serve with a cup of tea.

Richard Bertinet is a baker, chef and owner of the Bertinet Bakery and Kitchen in Bath. He is the author of five books on cooking and baking

Ravinder Bhogal

RHUBARB, ROSE AND PINK PEPPERCORN SOUFFLÉS

When I first met my husband, I thought I was through with love – but his silk-cut manners and gallantry flattered and persuaded me otherwise. His charm offensive included gestures considered old-fashioned nowadays by just about anyone under the age of 65, but he was ceremonious and sincere in them – he stood when I entered or departed a room, kissed the back of my hand in the French manner, and carried my bags as we traversed the bustling streets of London. And so, inspired by Voltaire's saying, "It is not enough to conquer; one must also know how to seduce", our campaign to win and to woo each other began.

He organised carousel dates that took us to romantic spots in the city and beyond, moonlit walks and stimulating telephone conversations about philosophy, religion and politics that started in the early evening and ended just as the light of the rising sun was flooding my bedroom. I, in return, dabbed on whispers of expensive perfume he had to lean in close to sniff. I wore dresses that encouraged him to stare and I'd fling back my head and let out strong, throaty laughs that displayed my powdered décolleté. Yet somehow my opponent stood undefeated, until one serendipitous afternoon, when quite unexpectedly I located his Achilles heel.

I'd been testing dessert recipes for my restaurant Jikoni, which had not yet opened its doors, and he surprised me with an unexpected visit. My kitchen was chaotic, but there on the worktop, laid out like bait, was a beauty pageant of pretty confections: a meringue roulade bursting with Roussillon apricots, orange blossom and cream, a wibbling lime leaf panna cotta built on faith and a whisper of gelatine, a rhubarb and pink peppercorn soufflé and a checkerboard of varying sponges, cakes and éclairs.

He picked up the soufflé and handled it as delicately as if it were a piece of rare, lost art. He raised it to the level of his chest and bent over to meet it with his nose to savour its scent. He dug a fork into its interior, and as his lips met the tines of the fork, he gasped. "It's like eating a cloud!" he exclaimed through a mouthful. "It's terrific!"

Sated, he fell onto the sofa – and fell for me.

For the soufflés

125g rhubarb

2 tbsp caster sugar

1 tbsp rosewater

1 tsp pink peppercorns, finely
crushed

1 tbsp cornflour

5 egg whites

40g caster sugar, plus extra for
dusting

softened unsalted butter and
caster sugar for greasing and
lining the ramekins

For the topping

3 tbsp roughly chopped
pistachios (I use the bright
green Iranian ones)

1 tbsp demerara sugar

1 tsp pink peppercorns, roughly
crushed

To garnish

a few dried rose petals

To make the soufflés, slice the rhubarb into 1cm chunks and put in a saucepan with the caster sugar and 1 tablespoon water. Bring to a simmer, stir gently and cook until tender.

Tip the cooked rhubarb into the bowl of a food processor along with all the sweet liquid and blitz to a purée. Pass through a fine sieve and then place back into the saucepan. Stir in the pink peppercorns and rosewater. Mix the cornflour with a tablespoon of water and mix to make a paste. Whisk it into the rhubarb purée and bring it to the boil, whisking constantly. Take off the heat and let it cool.

Preheat the oven to 200C/180C Fan/Gas 6.

Whisk the egg whites until frothy, then add the caster sugar and whisk to stiff peaks. Fold a third of the egg whites into the cooled rhubarb purée, then gently fold in the remaining egg whites – being careful not to beat out too much of the air. Grease 6 individual ramekin dishes with butter and coat the insides with caster sugar.

Fill the ramekins with the rhubarb soufflé mixture to the top, and level off with a palette knife. Clean the rims of your soufflé dishes by running your thumb around the edge of the ramekins – this will help your soufflés rise. Pop in the oven for 8 minutes.

In the meantime, mix together the pistachios, demerara sugar and pink peppercorns, then sprinkle over the surface of the soufflés and continue to cook for a further 2 minutes. Scatter with the rose petals and serve immediately with a spoonful of ice cream.

Ravinder Bhogal is a chef, a regular columnist for The Guardian *and founder of Jikoni restaurant in London's Marylebone*

Lily Jones

CHRISTMAS CARROT CAKE

I didn't grow up in a house with much baking or cooking, but yearly visits to my grandma sparked a lifelong interest in making cakes. My grandma was Irish and kind, with a sparkle in her eye. She always baked the same few things, always the same way and always to perfection. There was Irish soda bread, fruit scones and Victoria sandwich, filled with homemade blackcurrant or gooseberry jam from the bushes in her garden and dusted with icing sugar that she infused with a vanilla pod (which I thought was the most magical thing I had ever seen).

As soon as I was old enough to buy ingredients, I started experimenting for myself. This carrot cake was the first recipe I developed. It was around Christmas and I spent so long perfecting it that, for me, the smell of its ingredients in a pan on the stove still conjures up that time of year more than anything else. It's a wonderful cake to make in winter, because it requires a good amount of time standing over a bubbling mixture, stirring with a wooden spoon and with the most incredible, heart-warming aromas filling the room.

The wholegrain spelt in the recipe gives it a rich, nutty flavour, but you can substitute any wholemeal flour. All the spices are optional and you can choose to adjust the amounts or omit any of them you like. The cake doesn't need any icing, but it does go beautifully with a cream cheese frosting and a little zest of lime on top. It keeps well for over a week and improves with age as it softens and the spices come through.

SERVES 8

175ml runny honey

75ml water

120ml brandy

125g unsalted butter

250g peeled and trimmed organic carrots and/or any combination of parsnips, beetroots or sweet potatoes, all grated

90g raisins or stoned and chopped dates, or a mix of both

juice and finely grated zest of 1 orange

pinch of cinnamon

¼ nutmeg, finely grated

seeds from 4 cardamom pods, crushed

¼ tsp ground cloves

225g wholegrain spelt flour, sifted

2 tsp bicarbonate of soda

100g nuts (walnuts and pecans are good)

Grease two 23cm cake pans and line with baking parchment. Preheat the oven to 200C/180C Fan/Gas 6. Scatter the nuts on a roasting tray and toast in the preheated oven for 6-7 minutes, or until aromatic and just starting to brown. Roughly chop and put to one side.

Heat the honey, water, brandy, butter, carrot mix, dried and fresh fruit, citrus zest and juice, and spices together in a pan, stirring gently to melt the butter. Bring to the boil and cook for 6 minutes (set a timer). Take the mixture off the heat, remove the cloves if using, and allow to cool completely to room temperature.

Meanwhile, in a mixing bowl, whisk together the flour and bicarbonate of soda and stir in the crushed nuts.

Fold the wet mix into the dry. Divide the mixture between the two prepared cake tins and level out to the edges. Bake for 60-80 minutes, or until golden brown and a toothpick comes out clean. Remove from the oven and leave to cool in the tins for 10 minutes before turning out on to a wire rack to cool completely.

Sandwich the cake layers together with cream cheese frosting (if using), spread a layer on top and add lime zest if you're feeling fancy.

Lily Jones is the founder of Lily Vanilli Bakery in London and author of Sweet Tooth

Ravneet Gill

SELF-SAUCING DATE AND RICOTTA PUDDING

As a family we've always enjoyed proper puddings – those absolute classics you get in the supermarket: steamed syrup sponge, treacle tart, trifles, hot chocolate puddings. Nobody in my family baked when I was growing up, so the supermarket was always our friend. My mum tried baking a few times with packet mixes and even the Delia cookbook, but it never quite went to plan.

I was a really fussy eater as a child, though my pickiness never applied to sweet things. Often, at school dinner times, I'd forgo the savoury options and head straight for the hot sponge and jam pudding with custard. Eventually, I learnt to bake and started giving it a go myself. I'll never forget the magic of my first self-saucing pudding: re-reading the recipe over and over again and wondering if pouring hot liquid on top of cake batter was madness. And then, the sense of enjoyment and pleasure when it proved me wrong and came out baked just as it should be, with sauce on the bottom and a delicate sponge on top.

The recipe here is a slightly funkier update of the self-saucing idea. The ricotta in the cake batter makes it as light as air, while the date molasses forms the most addictive sauce at the bottom.

SERVES 4

- 40g unsalted butter
- 40g caster sugar
- 1 medium egg
- 50g self-raising flour
- 40g ricotta
- pinch of salt
- 30g date molasses
- 10g cornflour
- 110ml boiling water
- 10g demerara sugar

Preheat the oven to 200C/180C Fan/Gas 6.

Beat together the butter and sugar until light and creamy. Stir in the egg until well combined, then the flour and salt. Finally, stir in the ricotta. Dollop the mixture into a dish (I use a 13 x 18cm pie dish) and sprinkle demerara sugar on top.

Mix the date molasses with the cornflour and boiling water and pour over the pudding.

Bake in the oven for 17 minutes, or until a skewer comes out clean when inserted into the cake part (don't poke into the sauce layer or you won't be able to tell if it's cooked).

Serve with cold pouring cream – obviously.

Ravneet Gill is a pastry chef, baking columnist for The Telegraph *and judge on* Junior Bake Off

Tim Anderson

AUNT LISA'S PUMPKIN BREAD

We have a custom in America of giving classy or wholesome-sounding names to foods that really don't deserve them. One of my favourite side dishes growing up was something called "potatoes au gratin", which was made from a box of desiccated potato slices, rehydrated and cooked in milk along with a powdered sauce mix that had a flavour similar to cheese and onion crisps. It was tasty enough, but "au gratin"?

Similarly, anything containing mayonnaise can be called a "salad", even if it contains no vegetable matter. What we call tuna mayo and egg mayo in the UK are tuna salad and egg salad in the US. We even have dessert "salads", such as my Aunt Lynne's infamous "candy bar salad", which consists of chopped up Snickers bars, green apple and whipped cream, piled together in a bowl.

Another sneaky trick of American gastronomic vocabulary is the use of the word "bread" to mean anything bread-like in form. This includes things that are clearly cakes, such as my mother's "zucchini bread", which was a chocolate cake with grated courgettes baked into it (they imparted no taste or texture, but helped keep the cake very moist).

And, of course, my Aunt Lisa's pumpkin "bread", which she would make at Thanksgiving. Everybody has their favourite part of a Thanksgiving dinner and Aunt Lisa's pumpkin bread was the thing I looked forward to most. We had it with the savoury dishes, spread with extra butter, but it is definitely a cake nonetheless – an incredibly moist, sweet and luscious cake, with the richness of both tinned pumpkin and copious amounts of shortening. It is similar to a soft gingerbread, but less spicy and with a less treacly flavour.

I went to college in Los Angeles, and only came home for Thanksgiving a couple of times while I was there. One year, I told my mom how much I'd miss Aunt Lisa's pumpkin bread, and when she relayed this to my aunt, she sent me two loaves of pumpkin bread in the mail. They arrived amazingly intact, encased in several protective layers of clingfilm and foil. If memory serves me correctly, I devoured both of them in two days, sharing only a few precious slices with my friends.

You can make and serve this as a bread or a cake – it doesn't really matter. As a bread, I love it thickly spread with soft butter and sprinkled with sea salt. As a cake it would be lovely with a cream cheese frosting. And if you know someone out there, far away, who could use a little pumpkin-based care package, send them some. I know from experience that it travels pretty well.

The measurements are American – I know that's annoying, but when I converted this to metric weights it didn't turn out as well. Make sure all the ingredients are at room temperature.

⅔ cup shortening (or margarine)

2⅔ cups sugar

4 eggs

1 tin (400-425g) pumpkin (available online or at speciality food shops)

⅔ cup water

3⅓ cups plain flour

2 tsp baking soda

1½ tsp salt

½ tsp baking powder

1 tsp ground cinnamon

1 tsp ground cloves

Heat the oven to 180C/160C Fan/Gas 4. Line and butter two 23 x 13cm loaf tins. With an electric mixer, cream together the shortening and sugar until light and fluffy.

Beat in the eggs, followed by the pumpkin and water. When everything is well mixed, sift in the dry ingredients and continue to mix until a smooth batter forms.

Divide the batter between the two tins and bake in the centre of the oven for 45-60 minutes, until a toothpick inserted into the centre of the breads comes out clean.

Leave to cool completely before removing.

Tim Anderson is a chef and owner of two Nanban restaurants in London. He has written four books on Japanese cuisine and is a regular panellist on BBC Radio 4's Kitchen Cabinet

Simon Rogan

NANNY HINTON'S BREAD PUDDING

Most Saturday afternoons, my mum, dad, sister and I would get together with my aunties and cousins at the home of my Nan and Gran, who lived together in a Southampton suburb called Shirley Warren. We were all very close and did everything together. I was always filled with excitement at the prospect of meeting up with everyone and having fun.

All four generations would spend the afternoon catching up and enjoying each other's company, my cousins and me playing football in the garden and alternating between watching *World of Sport* with Dickie Davies and *Grandstand* with Frank Bough on the box. My Gran would be shouting at the Saturday afternoon wrestling right up until the start of the classified football results, when my Nan would check her pools coupons to see if she'd won. Early evening, shortly after she'd discovered that she hadn't, the table would be set with a buffet of sandwiches, cold meats, pies, pickles, salads, cheeses, trifle, chocolate biscuits and more. It was an absolute feast.

The star of the show was undoubtedly my Gran's bread pudding. The smell of it cooking was already wafting around the house when we arrived and we couldn't wait until evening when she would cut it into generous squares and add it to the buffet. I couldn't get enough of it – nor could the rest of the family – and usually, it was greedily devoured. But every now and then there would be some left over and we would get a little package to take home with us – a treat for later and a reminder of another special day.

SERVES 6-8

- 375g stale white bread, crusts removed, cut into small squares
- 425ml milk
- 2 medium eggs
- 90g suet
- 250g mixed dried fruit
- 125g dark brown sugar
- 1 tsp mixed spice
- grated zest of ½ lemon
- soft butter, for greasing
- caster sugar

Preheat your oven to 180C/160C Fan/Gas 4.

Put the bread pieces into a bowl, pour over the milk and leave to soak for at least 30 minutes.

Mash up the soaked bread mixture with a fork, then add the beaten eggs, suet, mixed dried fruit, brown sugar, mixed spice and grated lemon rind and give everything a good mix.

Grease a large roasting tin with plenty of soft butter and pour in the mixture.

Place in the middle of the oven and cook for 1½ hours.

When cooked and golden brown, take out of the oven and sprinkle with caster sugar. Leave to cool, then cut into squares – as big as you want.

Simon Rogan is an award-winning chef who owns several restaurants, including the three-Michelin-starred L'Enclume in Cumbria and Aulis in Hong Kong

Skye Gyngell

PEACH GALETTE

When I was a young girl, growing up in Australia in the late 1960s and early 1970s, stone fruit – and particularly peaches – symbolised the beginning of the summer holidays. On the last day of school, as a celebratory treat, my mother would bring home a box of peaches she had bought straight from an orchard south of Sydney. The fruit, freshly plucked from the trees and still warm from the sun, was sweet and heavenly scented.

As we munched into them, the delicious juices ran down our arms. We knew that, for the next few months, a time of complete freedom lay ahead of us and we roamed wild. That box of peaches was the signal that the summer had really begun.

MAKES A 20CM GALETTE

For the pastry

180g plain flour, chilled in the
fridge for 20 minutes

170g unsalted butter, cut into
cubes, well chilled

pinch of salt

1 tsp caster sugar

80ml chilled water

For the almond layer

3 tbsp ground almonds

3 tbsp plain flour

60g golden caster sugar

6 ripe peaches

3 tbsp golden caster sugar

juice of ½ lemon

50g demerara sugar

Start with the pastry. Combine the chilled flour, sugar and salt in a large mixing bowl. Put ⅓ of the cubed butter into the flour mixture and place in a food processor. Mix until the dough resembles coarse breadcrumbs (well-dispersed butter makes the dough light), then add the remaining butter and pulse in until the biggest pieces of butter are the size of small peas (these larger pieces of butter will make the pastry flaky).

Pour in the iced water and work until the dough just holds together. Do not pinch or squeeze the dough together, as this will overwork it.

Tip the crumby dough onto a large sheet of baking paper and lay another sheet on top. Using a rolling pin, roll the dough out between the paper to form a thick disc. Transfer to the fridge to rest for 15 minutes.

Preheat the oven to 200C/180C Fan/Gas 6. Roll the dough out on a cool, lightly-floured surface to a large, thin round, about 30cm in diameter. Lift the dough onto a sheet of baking parchment.

For the almond layer, toss together the ground almonds, flour and 60g sugar, then scatter over the pastry.

Slice the peaches in half and remove the stones as carefully as possible, so as not to tear the fruit. Slice each half into four pieces so each peach yields 8 slices. Toss with 3 tbsp sugar and the lemon juice. Arrange the pieces of peach in concentric circles, making a single layer of snugly touching slices and leaving a border of 5cm. Fold the edges of the pastry up over the fruit, crimping and tucking them gently as you go. Brush the pastry folds with the beaten egg and scatter over the demerara sugar.

Bake in the oven for 40-45 minutes or until the pastry is crisp and golden brown. For the best possible flavour and fragrance, eat within a couple of hours of making. Serve with crème fraîche or a scoop of vanilla ice cream.

Skye Gyngell is executive chef of Spring in London and Heckfield Place in Hampshire, and author of several award-winning cookery books

Ginny Rolfe

MUM'S SHERRY TRIFLE

Growing up in the 1970s in a family of six children was very interesting where food was concerned – there are so many wonderful, nostalgic memories. My mum would shop on a shoestring and the shopping bags would be raided before they were even unpacked. Our family meals were simple and would always feature potatoes and some sort of "meat", but the magic would happen with the homemade puddings.

Sherry trifle was always my dad's favourite and would be a masterpiece made over a couple of days. Fresh raspberries or strawberries came from my grandpa's garden or the pick-your-own farm (the abundance frozen so we could eat them during the winter). The sherry-soaked boudoir biscuits (why are they called that? The name still makes me smile) were often replaced with Weetabix biscuits because my siblings and I would have pinched them. In the words of Mr Kipling, surprisingly good. Then the wobbly raspberry or strawberry jelly, the silky Bird's Custard and softly cold vanilla whipped cream with hundreds and thousands, more berries and chocolate flakes crumbled over the top. Sometimes a bit of candied angelica made an appearance, too – but I didn't really understand why.

The way we could tell Mum's trifle was a good one was if it "squelched" when the spoon went in. So delicious and so very reminiscent of a Sunday afternoon.

I have written this recipe using packet jelly and Bird's Custard because that's what Mum always used and it would be wrong to change!

SERVES 10-12

100g boudoir biscuits (sponge fingers) or 6 Weetabix

100ml sweet sherry

250g fresh raspberries

300g fresh strawberries

2 x 135g pack of raspberry or strawberry jelly

35g Bird's Custard powder

2 tbsp golden caster sugar

2 tsp vanilla bean paste

600ml organic milk

600ml double cream

2 tsp vanilla bean paste

2 Cadbury's Flakes or 50g dark chocolate (70 per cent)

optional: hundreds and thousands, candied angelica

Arrange the biscuits or Weetabix on the bottom of a large glass trifle bowl (you can usually pick up beautiful crystal bowls from charity shops). Hull and slice the strawberries, reserving some for decoration, and scatter over the fingers with half of the raspberries then drizzle well with the sherry.

Tear up the jelly into cubes, pop in a heatproof measuring jug and add 600ml boiling water, stirring until all dissolved, then add 600ml of cold water. Pour over the sponge and fruit, place in the fridge and allow to set.

Prepare the custard by mixing the custard powder with the sugar and a little milk in a bowl, and mix until dissolved. Heat the remaining milk until nearly boiling, then add to the custard mix. Stir and return to the pan, whisking as it comes back to the boil and turns lovely and thick. Pour the custard into the bowl and allow to cool, stirring occasionally so the custard doesn't form a skin, then pour over the set jelly, spreading it out with the back of a spoon so the jelly is all covered.

Whip the double cream with the vanilla paste until you have soft peaks, then spoon over the layer of custard, creating peaks with the back of your spoon.

Finish the trifle by crumbling over the chocolate Flakes or, if you're feeling more upmarket, grate over the dark chocolate. Finally, decorate with the remaining raspberries and sliced strawberries, and for that true Seventies flourish, hundreds and thousands and candied Angelica if you fancy it.

Ginny Rolfe is head of food styling at the Jamie Oliver Group

Felicity Spector

RHUBARB COBBLER WITH CUSTARD

My dad took over all the cooking when I was about six and my mum was elected as a Birmingham Labour councillor – it meant she had lots of evening meetings and no time to cook. It was very rare in the 1970s for men to do any of the food shopping and cooking, but Dad took it on with enthusiasm. Like me, he had a sweet tooth and loved a proper hot pudding with custard – and they had a big enough back garden to grow some fruit.

I was not a big fan of rhubarb, it was a bit stringy and never sweet enough, except when dad made his rhubarb cobbler with its rings of rather biscuity scones on top. I remember the cinnamon flavour and the jammy, sticky bit around the edges where the fruit had caramelised against the dish. And the jug of Bird's Custard on the side. Hot custard on a hot pudding; cold custard (which always set rather solid in its stainless steel jug in the fridge) with cold leftovers the next day. I've made a version of it here with some almonds for added luxury – a warm, comforting dessert you can have with custard or cold the next day for breakfast with Greek yoghurt.

SERVES 4

500g rhubarb, trimmed and cut into 4cm pieces

100g caster sugar

2 tsp cornflour

juice of half an orange

For the cobbler topping

150g self-raising flour

50g ground almonds

½ tsp fine sea salt

½ tsp cinnamon

50g soft light brown sugar

100g cold butter, cut into 1cm cubes

150ml buttermilk (or same amount of milk with a squeeze of lemon juice)

1 tbsp demerara sugar

handful of flaked almonds

Preheat the oven to 200C/180C Fan/Gas 6.

Toss the sugar, cornflour and rhubarb together and place in a single layer in a non-reactive dish. Squeeze the orange juice over it and cover tightly with foil. Bake in the oven for 15 minutes until tender, but still holding its shape.

Let cool slightly and carefully transfer to a baking dish. Reduce the oven to 180C/160C Fan/Gas 4.

For the topping, tip the flour, almonds, cinnamon, salt and sugar into a food processor, add the butter and pulse a few times until it resembles breadcrumbs; a few bigger pieces of butter are fine. You can rub the butter in by hand.

Add the buttermilk and pulse again until it forms a sticky and coherent dough – don't overmix at this point.

Put spoonfuls of cobbler mix on top of the rhubarb – it will merge a little in the oven, so no need to be too precise – then sprinkle the demerara sugar and flaked almonds on top and bake for 35-40 minutes until the scone topping is golden brown and cooked through.

Serve with custard.

Felicity Spector is a food writer, influencer, and journalist at Channel 4 news

Paul A Young

MUM'S 5P FUDGE

Mum was always a fantastic sweet maker. She still is. It's where my love of sweets comes from. She used to make fudge in a saucepan so big that my head barely reached level with the top of it on the stove. At the time, I thought I would easily fit inside it. My mum would stand stirring and beating the bubbling gloop of condensed milk, butter and brown sugar, which emitted a buttery steam. It looked like the hot mud pools David Attenborough talked about on his nature programmes, but without the sulphurous smell.

On certain occasions, the fudge was destined for the local Ladies' Club, an organisation that, as a shy boy, I found both exciting and frightening. The club was our village version of the Women's Institute and my grandma attended its meetings at the community centre. The members held regular Christmas and summer events to raise money and selling homemade sweets was my mum's way of helping generate funds.

We would set up a small folding table at the entrance to the main hall with cupcake cases filled with toffee and small, clear bags of mum's amazing fudge. I was designated as shopkeeper and would sell each item for 5p. Inside, I was terrified and often snaffled bits of fudge without telling Mum. But I sold as many as I could and I remember everyone saying how wonderful it was.

This was my first taste of running a shop and selling homemade sweets. I didn't know that one day I would have shops of my own selling chocolate – and sometimes even the fudge I learnt to make from my mum.

4 level tbsp golden syrup
285ml condensed milk
285ml full fat whole milk
225g margarine
900g granulated sugar
¼ tsp cream of tartar
½ tsp vanilla extract

Grease a 23 x 33cm square-edged tin and line with baking parchment.

Put all the ingredients in a large saucepan and warm, stirring, until the sugar has dissolved.

Turn up the heat and boil quickly to 116C on a sugar thermometer (the soft ball stage).

Remove from the heat and beat well with a wooden spoon until it thickens and becomes grainy.

Pour into the tin and score the top into squares. Leave to cool and set. Cut through and eat.

Paul A Young is a chocolatier, pâtissier and broadcaster. He has written several books on cooking with chocolate

Grown-Up Drinks

Roger Phillips

SAUTERNES WITH TRUMPETS OF DEATH

In the 1980s, after my book, *Mushrooms and Other Fungi of Britain and Europe,* was first published, I was so carried away with enthusiasm that I thought I would travel the world studying mushrooms in different countries. My first stop was the USA, where I was asked to write *The Mushrooms of North America*. The plan was to spend the autumn mushroom season over the next five years in the USA to gather material for the book, starting in August and working through until the end of October. My wife Nicky and I had just had our first child, Phoebe, who, at the age of three months, travelled with us when we went to Boston to sign the contract.

Almost immediately, we made wonderful new friends, one of them Gerry Miller in Connecticut, who we ended up staying with for a week most autumns over the next few years. Gerry is an extraordinary man, who spends much of each year exploring the upper Amazon basin, living with tribes deep in the jungle. Like me, he is also keen on a tipple and on our visits we would often sit together in his kitchen sampling different wines in which he had submerged mushrooms.

My favourite was a Sauternes in which Gerry had immersed black trumpet mushrooms. He always referred to them as Trumpets of Death because of their black colour. The French name for them is the same: *trompettes de la mort*.

a handful of dried black trumpet
   mushrooms/trompettes

a half bottle of Sauternes (or
   similar dessert wine)

Put the dried mushrooms in a wide-mouthed jar and pour over the Sauternes.

Leave the mushrooms in the wine overnight so the flavour can infuse, then strain back into the bottle.

The late Roger Phillips was a photographer and author of botanical guides, who became a fungi expert and a guru for foragers. He died in 2021

Chris Edwardes

GERALDINE'S GINGER FIZZ

It was a hot and listless Ibizan afternoon when my good friend, the fiendishly knowledgeable gin expert Geraldine Coates, walked into Hidden, the bar I'd opened with my wife in 2011. I loved that place. It allowed me to be creative and innovative and we met some of our most wonderful friends there.

That particular day, we'd had the usual busy lunch, with crowded tables heaving with all kinds of delicious dishes and washed down with the customary flagons of good, crisp pale and moreish rosé.

Geraldine and her family were enjoying the easy fun of the place, same as everyone else. Only they stayed longer. When most people had gone home for their siestas, my friend shimmied up to the bar. "Go on, Chris," she said. "Make me the best gin cocktail in town – one that people will drink for years to come."

The challenge was set – and Geraldine's Ginger Fizz was born. She tried it and liked it so much, she had another, just to make sure. By that evening, it was on our house cocktail list and went on to become one of my signature drinks. To this day, it adorns the cocktail lists of numerous salubrious and dubious bars worldwide.

fresh ginger
50ml London dry gin
12.5ml Saint Germain elderflower liqueur
12.5ml elderflower syrup
25ml fresh lemon juice
5 turns of black pepper
50ml soda water

Cut five or six thin slices of peeled fresh ginger and smash to a pulp in the bottom of a cocktail shaker.

Add all other ingredients except the soda and fill the shaker with ice. Shake vigorously and dump everything into a large goblet. Fill with ice and add the soda, before garnishing with a lemon ring.

Chris Edwardes is the former head bartender at The Groucho Club and is now beverage director at Aura, Ibiza

Alice Lascelles

APRICOT SIDECAR COCKTAIL

Before I was a journalist, I was a musician of sorts – a job that mainly involved lugging my amp around London in the rain and playing to half-empty rooms that smelled of stale beer. Then, one day in 2007, the band I was in got a call from the White Stripes: they wanted us to support them on tour. We played Vienna, Rome, Milan, Paris and London. The Sidecar cocktail will always remind me of Paris.

It was a June night, and swelteringly hot. There were snails on the rider. And at one point there was definitely more than one person in the backstage shower. We careened through our set and then watched, from the side of the stage, as a sea of fists punched the air to "Seven Nation Army".

Afterwards, high on adrenaline and Jameson whiskey, we sped off in convoy to the Hemingway Bar at The Ritz. Jack White ordered the bar's signature, a Sidecar, made with cognac from 1865. It cost the best part of a grand. "This is for all the musicians who played tonight," he said, holding the drink aloft. "Everyone, take a sip." As it passed among us, the room fell silent for a moment.

How did it taste? I'm afraid I can't remember – by that stage my tastebuds were shot. But it's a memory I'll treasure forever. Even if we did miss our ferry home the next day.

This is my twist on the classic Sidecar, made with a little extra dash of stone-fruit liqueur.

SERVES 1

- 50ml cognac (1865 vintage optional)
- 25ml lemon juice
- 12.5ml triple sec
- 12.5ml apricot liqueur (a good-quality peach liqueur works well, too)

Shake hard with ice and strain into a frozen coupe. Spritz with a lemon twist and serve.

Alice Lascelles pens a regular drinks column for The Financial Times, *and has written two books on the subject,* 10 Cocktails: The Art of Convivial Drinking *and* The Cocktail Edit

A WHOLE HEAP OF GRATITUDE TO THE MOST ASTOUNDING & WONDERFUL COLLECTION OF INDIVIDUALS

This goregous book is in every part a technicolour realisation of the kindness, generosity and talent of an incredible collaborative community of people.

Together, they came together to make a wee gem of a storytelling cookbook. May it go forth into the world and do its work.

Thank you, first of all, to Lucas Hollweg and Clerkenwell Boy. Without you, this book would still be an idea rattling around in the far reaches of an ancient laptop. Your kindness and support have blown me away. You've picked up slack, reached out, made stuff happen, kept balls in the air and the juggernaut rolling.

Thank you, of course, to **MAGIC BREAKFAST** for taking on the most important task of all – working tirelessly to make sure that no child in the UK is too hungry to learn. I hope the money raised by this little book will help make your mission a reality.

Thank you to each and every one of our contributors. You are too many to mention individually, but your combined deluge of generosity has been overwhelming, not just in sharing your delicious recipes, but in revealing snapshots of your personal heritage. These gifts, they keep on giving, in every kitchen where they turn up, in every penny raised.

Thank you to Patsy and Tara, our wonderfully talented photographers, who shot the entire book in the course of five sweltering summer days. It is your relentless efforts and care that have made this book such a beautiful creation, the reality of which far out-strips our wildest dreams. Patsy, you were fair ready to burst in your final month of pregnancy, yet smashed through the almost-impossible shoot list with your giant sunshine smile. And Tara – not only did you throw your all into the photography, creating the most wonderful images, you also self-styled as Spreadsheet Supremo and kept us all on track.

Thank you to our passionate and brilliant stylists, Ginny and Rosie – two of the very best. It was a treat to watch you work, rustling exquisite beauty out of the simplest of dishes and transforming everything with the lightest of flourishes. And to the photographer's assistants and touchers-up, too, the oft unsung heroes of the final images.

Thank you to the mighty kitchen team, an evolving, revolving plethora of people who, throughout those heady studio days, came to lend hands, give their time and share their knowledge and care. Thank you for the relentless hours of chopping, blitzing, slicing, dicing, frying, braising, grilling, baking, washing up and cleaning down. The symphony of aromas that rolled through beautiful Stockwell Studios and out into the street told tales of great secrets happening inside. It was hot. It was intense. And it was fun, wasn't it?

Thank you to those who jumped on board at a moment's notice to pick up the myriad pieces: to Rick, for gathering up the remaining untamed words and making them sing harmoniously alongside the rest; and to Liz, for embracing all the visual elements that were thrown at you and placing them so elegantly and with such grace upon the page. Thanks to Charlie, our patient and steady agent – thank goodness for you. And to The Guild of Fine Foods, for your kind and generous support and for all that you do to encourage a world of Good Food.

Finally, a huge thank you to our publisher Steph and the team at Pavilion, for your belief that this book had legs and also for understanding that it has an important job to do.

Concept by Jane Hodson with
Lucas Hollweg and Clerkenwell Boy

Edited by Rick Jordan and Lucas Hollweg

Design by Elizabeth Edwards

Photography by Tara Fisher
and Patricia Niven except
page 19 Fingal Ferguson
pages 73 Chris Terry
page 89 Pierre-Louis Viel
page 100 Matthew Donaldson
page 127 Nassima Rothacker
page 192 Ed Schofield
page 233 Jonathan Lovekin
page 241 Jason Lowe

**Photographers' assistants and
retouching by** Sam Reeves, Jenni Colvin
and Isabel McCabe

Food styling by Ginny Rolfe,
Rosie Mackean and Jodene Jordan

Food stylists' assistants Melek Erdal,
Florence Blair, Julius Fiedler,
Flossie McAslan, Connie Simons and
Isabel McCabe

Kitchen assistants Mary Jo Sanchez,
Sharon Sharpe, Chris Warren and
Lily Sierra

Prop styling by Wei Tang

Prop stylist's assistant Saskia Sierra

Locations Stockwell Studio and
Kate Trelawny

Publishing Director Stephanie Milner
Design Director Laura Russell
Assistant Editor Ellen Simmons
Editorial Assistant Shamar Gunning
Design Assistant Lily Wilson
Production Manager Sarah Burke
Proofreader John Friend
Indexer Vanessa Bird

SUPPLIERS

Topham Street
www.tophamstreet.com

Kimbers' Farm Shop
www.kimbersfarmshop.co.uk

Alex Pole Ironwork
www.alexpoleironwork.com

Emsie Sharp
www.sharpglass.co.uk

Richard Pomeroy Porcelain
www.richardpomeroyporcelain.com

Fingal Ferguson Knives
www.fingalfergusonknives.com

The Flower Shop Bruton
www.theflowershopbruton.co.uk

Rushton's
www.rushtonsgreengrocer.co.uk

Infarm
www.infarm.com

Belazu Ingredient Co.
www.belazu.com

Swaledale Butchers
www.swaledale.co.uk

M. Moen & Sons
www.moen.co.uk

Bethnal Green Fish

Paul Rhodes Bakery
www.paulrhodesbakery.co.uk

Waitrose & Partners
www.waitrose.com

Pavilion
An imprint of HarperCollins*Publishers* Ltd
1 London Bridge Street
London SE1 9GF

www.harpercollins.co.uk

HarperCollins*Publishers*
Macken House
39/40 Mayor Street Upper
Dublin 1
D01 C9W8
Ireland

10 9 8 7 6 5 4 3 2 1

First published in Great Britain by Pavilion
An imprint of HarperCollins*Publishers* 2023

Copyright © Jane Hodson 2023

Jane Hodson asserts the moral right to be identified as
the author of this work. A catalogue record of this book is
available from the British Library.

ISBN 978-0-00-860360-1

This book is produced from independently certified FSC™
paper to ensure responsible forest management.

For more information visit: www.harpercollins.co.uk/green

Printed and bound by RRD in China

WHEN USING KITCHEN APPLIANCES PLEASE ALWAYS
FOLLOW THE MANUFACTURER'S INSTRUCTIONS

RECIPE CREDITS

p25: Adapted from *Jamie's Comfort Food* by Jamie Oliver, published by Penguin Random House © Jamie Oliver Enterprises Limited (2014 Jamie's Comfort Food)

p26: Extracted from *Home Kitchen* by Nathan Outlaw © Nathan Outlaw, 2017. Published by Quadrille.

p75: Recipe © Raymond Blanc

p128: Recipe © *Zoe's Ghana Kitchen* by Zoe Adjonyoh, published by Mitchell Beazley, 2017

p130: Recipe from *KITCHEN* by Nigella Lawson. © Nigella Lawson, 2010. Published by Chatto & Windus. Extract reproduced by permission of The Random House Group Ltd.

p218: extracted from *Asma's Indian Kitchen* by Asma Khan, published by Pavilion © Asma Khan 2018

p242: a version of this story and recipe originally appeared in *The Financial Times*.

p254: Extracted from *Risotto with Nettles* by Anna Del Conte, published by Chatto and Windus in 2006. © Risotto with Nettles 2006. Reproduced by permission of Sheil Land Associates Ltd.

p270: This recipe originally appeared in *The Telegraph*

With thanks to: Zoe Adjonyoh Paul Ainsw
Nieves Barragan Jane Baxter Fiona Becket
Rosie Birkett Raymond Blanc Neil Borthw
Xanthe Clay Felicity Cloake Chanta
Richard Corrigan Hélène Darroze Anna Del
Melek Erdal Gizzi Erskine Fingal Ferguson
Caroline Gilmartin Helen Goh Skye Gyng
Barny Haughton Ching He Huang Melissa
Mark Hix Jane Hodson Lucas Hollweg
Anna Jones Lily Jones Jacob Kenedy Tom
Merlin Labron-Johnson Alice Lascelle
Alastair Little David Loftus Henrietta Lo
Thomasina Miers Naved Nasir Andi Oliver
Tom Parker-Bowles Roger Philips Jose P
Mike Robinson Rachel Roddy Simon R
William Sitwell Nigel Slater Ed Smith
Rick Stein Rosie Sykes Melissa Thomps
Kate Trelawny Niki Segnit Stanley Tucci